Second Helpings

Second Helpings

Grandparenting

Hank Harbaugh

Ruth Harbaugh

Jim Harbaugh

Copyright © 2000 by Hank Harbaugh Ruth Harbaugh Jim Harbaugh.

Cover design by Brooke Barber

ISBN #:   Softcover   0-7388-6268-1

All rights reserved. No part of this book may be reproduced or transmitted in any form or by any means, electronic or mechanical, including photocopying, recording, or by any information storage and retrieval system, without permission in writing from the copyright owner.

This book was printed in the United States of America.

To order additional copies of this book, contact:
Xlibris Corporation
1-888-7-XLIBRIS
www.Xlibris.com
Orders@Xlibris.com

CONTENTS

THE SOUND OF LOVE

ONE	17
TWO	19
THREE	21
FOUR	23
FIVE	25
SIX	27
SEVEN	29
EIGHT	31
NINE	33

LESSONS LEARNED

TEN	35
ELEVEN	37

TWELVE	39
THIRTEEN	41
FOURTEEN	43
FIFTEEN	45
SIXTEEN	47
SEVENTEEN	49

NAMES AND PLACES

EIGHTEEN	51
NINETEEN	53
TWENTY	56
TWENTY-ONE	58
TWENTY-TW0	60
TWENTY-THREE	62

GIVE AND TAKE

TWENTY-FOUR	64
TWENTY-FIVE	66
TWENTY-SIX	68

TWENTY-SEVEN	70
TWENTY-EIGHT	72
TWENTY-NINE	74
THIRTY	76
THIRTY-ONE	78

SOCIALIZING

THIRTY-TWO	79
THIRTY-THREE	81
THIRTY-FOUR	83
THIRTY-FIVE	85
THIRTY-SIX	87
THIRTY-SEVEN	89
THIRTY-EIGHT	91
THIRTY-NINE	93
FORTY	95
FORTY-ONE	97
FORTY-TWO	99

LOVE AND LOSS

FORTY-THREE 101

FORTY-FOUR 103

FORTY-FIVE 105

FORTY-SIX 107

FORTY-SEVEN 109

FORTY-EIGHT 111

FRUSTRATION

FORTY-NINE 113

FIFTY 115

FIFTY-ONE 117

FIFTY-TWO 119

FIFTY-THREE 121

UNEXPECTED GIFTS

FIFTY-FOUR 123

FIFTY-FIVE 125

FIFTY-SIX 128

FIFTY-SEVEN 130

FIFTY-EIGHT 132

FIFTY-NINE 134

SIXTY 136

EXPERIENCE TEACHES

SIXTY-ONE 138

SIXTY-TWO 140

SIXTY-THREE 142

SIXTY-FOUR 144

SIXTY-FIVE 146

SIXTY-SIX 148

JOY AND PAIN

SIXTY-SEVEN 150

SIXTY-EIGHT 152

SIXTY-NINE 154

SEVENTY 156

SEVENTY-ONE 158

SEVENTY-TWO 160

ENTERTAINING

SEVENTY-THREE 162

SEVENTY-FOUR 164

SEVENTY-FIVE 166

SEVENTY-SIX 168

SEVENTY-SEVEN 170

SEVENTY-EIGHT 172

ROLE MODELS

SEVENTY-NINE 174

EIGHTY 176

EIGHTY-ONE 178

EIGHTY-TWO 180

EIGHTY-THREE 182

EIGHTY-FOUR 184

EIGHTY-FIVE 186

EIGHTY-SIX	188
EIGHTY-SEVEN	190
EIGHTY-EIGHT	192
EIGHTY-NINE	194
NINETY	196

HELLO AND GOODBYE

NINETY-ONE	198
NINETY-TWO	200
NINETY-THREE	202
NINETY-FOUR	204
NINETY-FIVE	206
NINETY-SIX	208
NINETY-SEVEN	210
NINETY-EIGHT	212
NINETY-NINE	214
ONE-HUNDRED	216

DEDICATION

To all grandparents' children, who take their turn and make this new role possible, and, of course, to grandchildren, especially Alexander and Nicolas.

"PERFECT LOVE SOMETIMES DOES NOT COME UNTIL THE FIRST GRAND CHILD"

WELSH PROVERB

ONE

HANK

"My children, our love should not be just words and talk, it must be true love, which shows itself in action." (1 John 3.18)

Love is surely the hardest word in the English language to define. I recently read an interview with Julia Sweeney. She was discussing her performance film *God Said, Ha!*, and she said that she disliked and mistrusted the word *love* because, when used, it so often meant something other than love. It might mean, "You provide me with security," or "I am needy, so say 'I love you' back so I can be reassured," or "I want something from you, and I will say anything to achieve my selfish goal." Part of me, maybe more than a part, agrees with Julia's suspicion. As an exercise in word clarification, I used to ask my teenage students to define love and listened as they tied themselves in knots trying to get it right. It was always an interesting discussion and little was resolved.

Last October Alexander, my older grandson, was visiting. It was his final outing with me on one of those perfect, golden days when I don't know whether to enjoy being deliciously toasted or turn the air on in the car. He was strapped in the back seat, out of sight. We were stopped at a light, and he had said nothing for several minutes. I thought perhaps he was experiencing sun-induced doze-off when I heard, "I love you, Grandpa." His words were touching, unexpected, and totally natural. "I love you too, Alexander," I responded quite simply, and we were both silent again.

Five minutes later we were rolling and rearranging pumpkins outside a produce market while waiting for the oil to be changed. Making sure that none of the store's stock was being damaged by a four-year old, I was both watchful and nervous, hoping that the employees could not see what we were doing. If I saw the least frown, I would have immediately pulled Alexander away and stopped the fun. I grant that I shouldn't have been letting him reconfigure someone else's for-profit pumpkins. His parents would surely not have allowed it. But I did. And I'd do it again simply because he was having such a grand time.

It is difficult to experience pure love with another adult, as Julia so eloquently expressed, but not with a child. With grandparents, a grandson knows his interests come first. One of the main reasons why a grandson loves you is because you will let him explore out to, and sometimes even beyond, the edges of acceptable behavior while keeping him from danger.

TWO

RUTH

"When a thing is funny, search it carefully for a hidden truth." (George Bernard Shaw)

Each time we visit our grandsons it gives me great pleasure to spend lots of time reading to them. As an elementary teacher I have a long list of favorite books that are fun to share. One that we have read an endless number of times is *Chicka Chicka Boom* by Bill Martin. The rhythm is pleasing, and Alexander used to love to repeat the alphabet letters with me. He has outgrown the book, but Nicolas hasn't.

One evening years ago Alexander and I were lying in bed upstairs with the door open enjoying chanting the alphabet together when he had an unexpected hiccup. We stopped. Both surprised, we stared at each other. Then we laughed simultaneously, paused, and laughed again. I continued with the next page in the book. But Alexander wanted to prolong the moment. He hiccuped again. "Pick-ups," Alexander said, interrupting me with enthusiasm and misnaming his gastric condition. We covered our faces with the book and giggled some more. With each subsequent hiccup Alexander's eyes got wider and wetter from laughter. My voice rang with delight at the anticipation of the next, even more explosive hiccup.

Soon we could hear Alexander's dad coming. As he approached the door, I quickly closed the book, gave Alexander a quick goodnight kiss, and headed for the stairs. I knew it was bedtime by his parents' rules.

All of us have shared a treasured moment like this with a friend or loved one. A slight gesture by a stranger or a facial expression on an acquaintance might bring this moment to mind. At the time it seemed like the most ordinary of events. Under other circumstances, hiccups might be a cause for anxiety or an annoyance. But looking back on this experience I realize that a special bond embraced us at the time we laughed together. Film director, James L. Brooks, writing in the New York Times, Tuesday, March 9, 1999, said, "What makes people laugh is a mystery." So are ordinary moments, I suppose, which become special.

THREE

JIM

"Thus says God, who created you, . . .who formed you, . . .'Do not be afraid, . . .I have called you by your name, you are mine.'" (Isaiah 43:1)

My grandnephews are named Alexander and Nicolas. When people hear their names together, they wonder if my family is Russian, or somehow involved in the sad fate of the last Tsar and his Tsarina. Actually, my niece Lisa, who married into a French speaking family, just liked the sounds of those names, partly because they worked in both English and French, important in a bicultural and bilingual mix. By the way, "Nicolas"—no h—is the French spelling, which he'll be reciting to travel agents, tellers, and other name verifiers his whole life.

My niece also informed me that for some reason in France one is required to give a child four names. As a result, both boys have quite a few monikers, but I think all of their names reflect who they are, or perhaps who they may grow to become.

Take Alexander, for instance. His three given names are Alexander René Moana. As the firstborn of his generation in both families, his chosen name had to have a certain princely quality. One which chimes with Alexander the Great seemed perfect. As I noted at his baptism, "René"—"the reborn one"—seems appropriate for a boy who has brought so much new life into his family, and especially into my life. The world starts all over again with grandchildren. Finally, "Moana" is an *hommage* to another strain in his ancestry—his paternal grandmother comes from the South Pacific, namely New Caledonia, and Alexander's father Stanley was born in Tahiti and given that unlikely and hardly exotic name for family reasons. I hope that this strand brings Alexander a love of nature and a Gauguinesque freedom from some of the hangups he may have inherited from his German and Irish ancestors (people like me).

His younger brother's names are, first, Nicolas, the name of a legendary early Christian bishop, renowned for his generosity. His second name is Louis, after an uncle in France, but of course also after the saint-king of France, after whom the Missouri city and the university where his parents met is named. His third name—well, what can I tell you? I would have loved his brother and him under any name. But I take great pride and joy in the fact that Nicolas's third name is James.

FOUR

HANK

"Life is much more important than food, and the body much more important than clothes." (Luke 12.23)

When Nicolas was five months old, he made his first visit to St. Louis. His godfather/uncle Matthew and Matt's wife Jennifer hosted a party to introduce three generations on both sides of the family to the new arrival. The noise and confusion in the hall as we all greeted each other caused Nicolas to become agitated. There were too many strange faces and too much noise for a baby just getting used to this world. Sobbing piteously, he needed, not introductions, but instant removal. I carried him upstairs, found the office, closed the door, and eased into the rocking chair. As I held his ear against my heart, I softly sang my favorite song to him over and over. The sobs subsided, becoming grunts. Then all was silent as he drifted to sleep.

Convinced that I was the only one present, except for his mother, who could have accomplished this feat, I congratulated myself. As others came upstairs to relieve me, I waved them away.

This totally delightful situation reminded me of Alexander's baptism when the cold water in the face in strange surroundings caused a similar storm. Again, it was I alone who could bring comfort and restore calm. I smilingly concluded that this is what grandfathers, whose movements have been slowed by time, are for.

I rocked Nicolas contentedly and listened to the party in full swing below. I could hear the sounds of chair scraping and plates and utensils being put to use. I fervently hoped that everyone dining below would forget where the main attraction was and dreaded the feet on the stairs, the gentle knock, and another offer of relief. I wanted only to extend this experience, which would never come again in quite the same way, as long as I possibly could.

It wasn't until this time that I became truly aware of the length of a moment and the brevity of a life. I began counting the number of people downstairs in the next generation, that is, the next for me to enter. Two! I felt suddenly mortal, smacked in the face by reality. I had become, without anticipation, the older generation. The only one left was *oldest*. Then.... But it was OK. I held the future against my heart.

FIVE

RUTH

"Without music, life would be a mistake." (Friedrich Nietzsche)

Playing the piano with my grandsons on the bench sitting quietly, or not so quietly, on either side of me has always brought me extreme pleasure, but that pleasure doesn't last very long. Children seek movement. They must wiggle.

Both boys like to touch the keys. When the song is a favorite, Alexander will sing out with gusto. Nicolas watches with a big smile on his face and hums along. He wants the song to be repeated over and over again. When action is called for, stomping, tiptoeing, or beating on a pot, Alexander and Nicolas will march around the living room often forgetting to sing along. Alexander gets under the piano and manipulates the pedals. Nicolas pulls himself up on the sofa and rolls around when the music inspires him to intense action or he wants a larger share of attention.

Most of the board books (the thick ones for the very young who would maul flimsy paper) that Nicolas has been exposed to have been handed down from his brother. However, there is one board book that Ali (my favorite of Alexander's nicknames) has still not outgrown and both boys will focus on. Raffi put the words of the song *Wheels on the Bus* into story form, and he uses pictures to evoke actions. Children anticipate the repeating words, which instinctively starts hand and body movement. The pictures use vivid colors, and the pages show things little children know such as wheels, driver, people, horn, baby, and parents.

There are many other equally fine books that combine words from familiar songs and storybook format. They are wonderful tools for encouraging a grandchild to be an active observer/listener. Sometimes I put my finger under the words that I am reading so that the boys can see that I am reading from left to right on the page. When I do this, Alexander, three years older than his brother, wants to predict what will appear on the next page.

Alexander and Nicolas like songs that have finger plays as well. *I'm a Little Teapot, Two Little Birds, Where is Thumbkin?, Johnny Works With One Hammer, Here is the Bee-hive, Join in the Game, Ten Little Indians, She'll Be Coming Around the Mountain, Eency-weency Spider* are favorites.

If you do not play the piano but would like a book to help with finger movements, Marc Brown has compiled an excellent collection of *Hand Rhymes*.

To enhance the music-reading-action connection, tapes and CDs can be purchased that help children learn what will surely become their favorite songs. *The Ultimate Kids Song Collection* with one-hundred-and-one sing-a-longs from Wonder Workshop, Inc. comes to mind.

SIX

JIM

God says, "I will never forget you. See, I have branded you on the palms of my hands." (Isaiah 49: 15-16)

I once heard someone say during a spiritual discussion that, "God has no grandchildren." I did not have the opportunity at the time to request an explanation, and I have pondered the comment since. I'm still not sure what the speaker meant by this—maybe that we're as close to God as children are to parents. Maybe he meant that God is only and always a primary care provider. In any event, my first thought was, "How sad for God!"

God can be thought of in a lot of different ways, of course. But I find thinking of God as a grandparent especially attractive. If there's one thing that characterizes the love of a grandparent for a grandchild, it's the lack of ego on the grandparent's part. This lack of ego—or, to put it another way, this surplus of love—has several roots. First, parents legitimately feel that they are judged by other adults on the basis of the behavior of their children, which unavoidably brings more ego into that relationship. Second, if you're old enough to be a grandparent, with any luck you're also old enough to have grasped that what other people think of you—on the rare occasions when they think of you at all—isn't very important.

Whatever its source, grandparental love is often rich and

unstinting. And if this derives from lack of ego, then surely God can be assumed to love this way. God has no ego at all, in the sense of something that needs to be defended or demonstrated or proved. This is what we mean when we say simply that God *is* love. Grandparents come closer to incarnating a loving God than just about any other human beings in a child's experience.

SEVEN

HANK

"Children are fortunate if they have a father who is honest and does what is right." (Proverbs 20.7.0)

My Mother had blue eyes, shockingly blue. My wife, my children, and I have hazel to brown. My son-in-law is of French-Polynesian descent and has the darkest eyes of all of us, including his parents.

Nicolas was born in January with blue eyes. Not uncommon. I heard about them often when I spoke to his mother or father on the phone. But from February, when I went to help out for a few days and attend his baptism, through May I did not see him.

Lisa announced a visit in St. Louis to introduce Nicolas to the extended family, who had not yet seen him. On the second day of the month I was in the airport and at the gate early, happily ready to greet the entire family as they deplaned.

They came forward in a family unit and looked surprisingly calm and refreshed despite the long flight. Lisa, knowing me well, immediately handed over my new grandson.

I studied his face. Nicholas looked quite different from four months ago. Of course he did. Newborns appear fragile, somewhat misshapen, and they sleep like the very, very old as if the very act of living is an exhausting effort. Now he seemed alert, already a baby instead of an infant, and ready to take on the world.

But what I began to focus on was not his general appearance but his blue eyes, shockingly blue. Memory kicked in. He had the eyes of my Mother, who had been dead for twenty-five years. Long dormant glimpses of the past starring my caring mother came to the surface, and I prayed that Nicolas would keep these eyes for his entire lifetime.

But then I greeted his Brother Alexander with his eyes like dark chocolate syrup and his Father Stanley with eyes even darker, two black holes without a bottom.

I looked down at Nicolas's true blues. "Little chance," I sighed as I helped them gather their carry-ons so that we might head for the carousel.

Stanley kissed his wife and sons goodbye.

I didn't understand. I asked, "What's this all about?"

"I'm not staying," he explained. "I just flew with them to help Lisa with the boys."

It was true. He turned around, got back on the plane, and flew directly back to Vancouver. Four more hours in the air.

I headed out of the terminal gripping my new grandson with both arms. I was still amazed at the blue, blue eyes that were wondering who I was and studying me suspiciously.

All of a sudden I didn't want him to keep them. I wanted them, over time, to become the eyes of his Father.

EIGHT

RUTH

"The God to whom little boys say their prayers has a face very like their mother's." (James M. Barrie)

At eighteen months Nicolas spent most of his time with his mother. The first person to greet him in the morning and the one to tuck him in at night with frequent feedings in between, Lisa was the center of his universe. During this period Nicolas stayed relentlessly close and endlessly tried to get her attention, especially when she was on the phone or dealing with his brother. His devotion was restrictive and possessive during this stage of development, and she left him very little with sitters. She knew that this mother fixation, right on schedule, would pass because she had experienced the same with Alexander.

A book that picks up on this emotion in the very young child is called *Are You My Mother?* by P.D. Eastman. The book was first published in 1960 and is still in print; and as you might expect, the dedication reads, "To my mother." The story involves a baby bird looking for his mother, who is away searching for food. He travels from place to place seeking information about her from other animals.

When Nicolas stayed with us during this period and his mother left for a few hours, I tried to keep him very busy. If the separation was to extend past his nap or bedtime, I would attempt to read this story. I say *attempt* because I would always end up just showing the pictures to him and making a few comforting comments per page because Nicolas was still too young to listen to the full text. But he clearly understood the main idea of the book. He would vocalize the names of the mamma and the baby bird, and he always smiled when he saw the final page with them back in the nest together.

As a grandchild enters school, whether it's preschool or kindergarten, a book called *The Kissing Hand* by Audrey Penn can help him or her make the transition from home to independence. Mother Raccoon tells Chester, "Now whenever you feel lonely and need a little loving from home, just press your hand to your cheek and think, Mommy loves you. That kiss will jump to your face and fill you with toasty warm thoughts." What may sound like too much sentimentality to an adult is just the right amount for a young child feeling separation anxiety from a loved one. Even adults experience this emotion, but we call it heartache, the blues, or a period of depression.

NINE

JIM

"Does a woman forget her baby at her breast, or fail to cherish the child of her womb? Yet even if she forgets, I will never forget you." (Isaiah 49:15)

I left Alexander's house in a hurry. It was one of those special occasions when the whole complement of grandparents and I were there. Summer plans were about to scatter us in many directions. It was early evening. I yet had to drive the three hours from there to my home in Seattle, so I stayed just long enough to finish our family supper. With so far to drive, and so many people to bid farewell to, I walked past Alexander and just patted him briefly on the shoulder.

Outside, I threw my overnight bag into the car and was preparing to peel out of the driveway when I felt someone's eyes on me. I turned around and looked toward the house. Alexander, alone, had come out of the air-conditioned indoors and stood there, sad and accusing. I turned off the engine, stepped out of the car, stooped down and asked, "What's up, Alexander?"

He said softly, "You forgot me!"

He was mostly right, given the fact that I had lavished less attention on him than I had on others. What could I do but hug him and say what is one of the truest things about me. I said, "I'm so sorry!"

He was not appeased.

"I didn't forget you. I never forget you. I think about you all the time."

He now returned my hug and then, after this proper goodbye, I drove off with the image of a grinning Alexander in my rear view mirror. But while I was smiling and driving and waving, I was thinking to myself, "This is exactly what God says to us in Isaiah—God never forgets us either. God thinks about us all the time. If I can do this with Alexander, as distracted and self-absorbed as I usually am, then God, who is neither, really and truly never forgets."

As so often happens, Alexander's words kept me warm and grateful all the way home. This experience gave me a deeper understanding of relationships, and it also taught me to be especially careful when it comes time to say goodbye.

TEN

HANK

"Children have more need of models than of critics." (Petrus Jacobus Joubert)

Stan set his new camera on its tripod in our backyard. An obsessed amateur photographer, he was about to practice on a fabulous subject, Ruth's garden. This sunny, warm morning was an endangered species since it was now October. Soon the mums and pansies would be covered, first by leaves and then by snow.

Alexander began to climb the forbidden wall, and I rushed over to grab him in case of a misstep. Perhaps because he trusted me to watch, Stan didn't react to the danger. Then too, he was engrossed in his project.

I flashed on a scene a few years before when we had climbed a mountain in France. At the top we rested while three generations of family had lunch. Too awed by the view to want food or wine, Ruth and I sat at the edge with our feet on a narrow ledge while we admired Lake Annecy far, far below. Stan climbed past us to talk and turned to face us. The front of his shoes had a perch, but the backs hung over space. He let go of the overreaching branch, and Ruth and I both grabbed for him. He laughed.

When Alexander was safely down, I watched Stan remove one of several lenses from his bag. He spoke of the two new ones he would buy when he could afford them. I looked down and was impressed by the ones he already owned. They were neatly arranged, and I flashed on his organized array of tools in the hallowed work area back home.

I recalled Alexander's compulsion to gather pine cones under the tree in our front yard. He placed them in the back of his play car until it was full and we had to get a bag to continue. He would not rest until every one was gathered and neatly stored.

"Oh, man!" Stanley said. "There's something on this lens." He polished and polished it until it gleamed. I remembered the day he dove into the lagoon on Moorea time after time in order to cleanse a living reef of objects carelessly tossed overboard. Working tirelessly for most of an afternoon, he made a large pile of bottles, plastic bags, and other flotsam on the beach while the rest of us sunbathed.

I thought of the time Alexander and I waited outside Walmart for the others to finish shopping. "Oh, man!" Alexander exclaimed as he ran over and picked up a plastic cup that someone had thrown down. He put it in a trashcan and then reached down for cigarette butts. I prevented this but could not dissuade him from policing the rest of the area.

Like Father....

ELEVEN

Ruth

"You know children are growing up when they start asking questions that have answers." (John J. Plomp)

Breakfast is an event for Nicolas and Alexander. Fifteen hours without food for growing boys gives new meaning to *break a fast*, and the boys are usually hunting in the refrigerator for something to tide them over while we check out our choices. The ultimate foods for them are pancakes or waffles. Mom has special recipes for both. Many mornings Alexander will climb up on the kitchen counter to help mix the pancake batter with a spatula or spoon. He watches intently as it goes into the pan and begins to bubble. Mom flips them, and the excitement mounts with the familiar smell. "Are they ready?" he asks repeatedly.

Meanwhile Nicolas in his highchair is given a few blueberries so that his grunting and pointing doesn't distract the cook. I am setting the table, getting the orange juice and syrup ready. Never quite fast enough, it is time to come to our places.

Tomie DePaola's *Pancakes for Breakfast* is a wordless book with pictures that takes children through the process of making pancakes. The author starts with the basic ingredients. The reader sees a woman, perhaps a grandmother, gather eggs from a chicken's nest. "Why do chickens lay eggs in a nest?" Alexander asked the first time we studied the book.

The reader then sees the same woman milking a cow to fill a pitcher. "How do you milk a cow?" Alexander wanted to know. On the next page a churn fills with cream to make butter. "How do you make cream into butter, Grandma?" he wondered aloud as I flashed on watching my actual grandmother making butter this way when I was my grandson's age. An unpredictable occurrence at the end of the story surprises the reader. The lady solves a problem by joining her neighbors. A meal begins. "If at first you don't succeed, try again," is the ultimate message on the final page. This may be a cliché to adults, but it could be a new thought to a small child.

Other valuable lessons can be taught with books like *Pancakes for Breakfast*. When Alexander and I came back to this book without any words for the second time, I asked him, "What word is important for this page?" Alexander studied the picture and decided from the many visual clues what word was significant to him. "Milk," he called out. "Butter," he added. I wrote these two words on separate pieces of Post-it Correction and Cover-up Tape and attached them to the page and individual picture. This technique is called *adding meaningful text* and teaches that words result from visual observation of objects, many of which are seen by children only in pictures. During a final reading we looked at each picture and tried to say the words on the tape. The tapes come off easily and do not harm the book.

TWELVE

JIM

"Listen, brothers and sisters: it was those who are poor according to the world that God chose, to be rich in faith and to be heirs to the kingdom which God promised to those who love God." (James 2:5)

In many religious traditions, there's some kind of ritual for welcoming the newborn child to the community and to the world. As a symbol of allegiance Jewish families circumcise male offspring on the eighth day after birth (Brit Milah). Before the ceremony the boy is placed upon the Prophet Elijah's seat, and during it he is named. In many Christian communities, baptism is the common rite. I was struck by who showed up uninvited—at least by us, perhaps not by God—at the christenings of my two grandnephews, and how appropriate those guests were when I consider the kind of human beings the boys are turning out to be.

On Alexander's christening day, a bright, crisp afternoon in November, there was, coincidentally, a Jesuit novice praying in the otherwise empty church where our family had come to welcome Alexander into the world. When this distracted novice realized what we were up to, he offered to leave; but I encouraged him to stay, to be, in fact, the Designated Prayer. The young novice went on to become a well-regarded professor of philosophy, and somehow the grandeur of this seems to fit Alexander, who, as the firstborn in his immediate family and the first baby in the extended family in more than twenty-five years, was special from the first.

    Like many second children, Nicolas is much more easygoing than his big brother. So the guests at his early February christening seemed as fitting as Alexander's guest was at his. It turned out that the baptismal party was delayed a little in getting to the church for Nicolas's big moment by weather and traffic. Typically earthy and totally typical for a newborn, he pooped right after the closing of the final button on his christening gown, and the whole rig had to be disassembled and reconstructed. I was waiting in the church, and when the party didn't come at the appointed time, I decided to look on the parking lot. As I neared the front door, I heard the sounds of the 1980's rock group Queen's "Bohemian Rhapsody" just outside. It turned out to be four homeless men, complete with shopping cart and a mutt-on-a-rope. The assistant pastor had told them that they could stay there out of the rain overnight. They moved on to another, hopefully warmer, destination just as the family cars started showing up, rather to my relief. Nicolas's stylish French grandmother would have been startled ("Bonjour, Monsieur Wino!") had the overnighters stayed to greet the newcomers, and three-year-old Alexander was, at this stage, sometimes afraid of big, barking dogs.

    But I thought this fulsome foursome was an appropriate group to greet Nicolas, just like the shepherds who greeted the baby Jesus in the Gospel of Luke (the Wise Men are in a whole different gospel). I think God sent wisdom as a christening gift to Alexander; but to Nicolas God sent the equally wonderful gift of compassion. Time will tell whether or not the gifts have been returned.

THIRTEEN

HANK

"Life, for most of us, is a continuous process of getting used to things we hadn't expected." (Unknown)

He was afraid of his own shadow! Four-year old Alexander and I had been chasing each other in late afternoon when I noticed that he was casting a long, thin pencil of shade on the sidewalk. Since it's continuous fun to be the first teacher, I laughingly pointed it out to him, hoping that he had never really noticed this phenomenon. I was right. He looked down, saw what I was pointing at, and became immediately uncomfortable. His body language stated quite clearly that he wanted only to get away from this alien formation. I picked him up to eliminate the source of his anxiety. It was not going to be a chance for me to instruct about angles and light after all because, instead, we were experiencing an unsettling threat.

Yes, this child who took nightly walks with me carrying a flashlight into absolute darkness to find rocks that were clearly visible during the day, did not want to be told about his shadow. I set him down in the shade of a tree, and as he edged toward sunlight, I quickly distracted him with a mock tackle. Wrestling him to the grass, I rid him of his eerie companion.

Someone else apparently had the fun of teaching him about shadows, or he simply matured, because months later we played the game of stepping on each other's shadow without upset.

When children exhibit fear of the completely natural, our tendency is to exclaim, "How silly! It's only a shadow." Or a dog. Or a siren. But we must hold our tongues. A child's life is quite full of totally new experiences, some of which are bound to be unsettling. They decide which ones are, not us.

Fourteen

Ruth

"Praise does wonders for the sense of hearing." (Unknown)

One fall evening I introduced Alexander to a delightful book about owls. It turns the subject into real adventures in both listening and learning. Jane Yolen's *Owl Moon* has become a page-turner that he never seems to tire of. In it Pa and the narrator, a young girl, go out on a winter night to look for owls. They take flashlights along. Cupping their ears, they listen for sounds. A train whistle blows, and the dogs answer by howling. Feet crunch in the snow. Pa says to his daughter, "If you want to go owling, you have to be quiet," but then he calls out, 'Who-who-who-who-whooooo!" Within a few minutes they hear a response from the trees (at this point Alexander, listening intently to this story for the first time, spontaneously made owl sounds). The Great Horned owl flies over the father and daughter. Amazed, they turn their flashlights on it, and for one brief moment the humans and the bird stare at each other until the owl flies back into the forest. The story ends with Pa observing, "When you go owling you don't need words or warm or anything but hope. The kind of hope that flies on silent wings under a shining Owl Moon."

Outside of Alexander's bedroom window are some giant trees. An owl lives there. Sometimes Alexander is afraid when he hears the big WHOOO sound from among the mysterious branches at night. *Owl Moon* doesn't make the bird seem scary but simply a natural, nocturnal creature looking for food. When we talked about being scared, Alexander admitted that the sound was frightening to him because he thought that the unseen bird might fly to his window.

Understanding the owl's habits, I hoped, would make his own nighttime visitor a lot less frightening. Consequently, we looked at some non-fiction owl books and talked about the habits of these birds, like killing small animals such as rats. We searched for pellets in the woods nearby. I had one in my pocket just in case we didn't find any. When we didn't, I took the pellet out and showed it to him. "What are pellets?" I asked Alexander. He didn't know. I handed it to him and encouraged him to break it open. He pulled it apart and we carefully examined what was inside. We found compacted hair and bones that the owl spit out after he had eaten a rat. Alexander didn't fully understand what he was seeing, but he did touch the contents with curiosity. "Pellets won't hurt you," I explained, taking some of it in my hand. We talked about the word *nocturnal*. Through this experience I believe that Alexander gained respect for the role owls play in nature.

The following summer we saw live owls up close at Grant's Farm in St. Louis. The raptor show lets a Barn Owl and a Great Horned Owl fly free over a large audience. Alexander loved it. With so much exposure to these birds he was relaxed about both these owls and the one in his backyard.

FIFTEEN

JIM

Jacob was afraid and said, "How awe-inspiring this place is! This is nothing less than a house of God; this is the gate of heaven!" (Genesis 28:17)

In a previous essay I mentioned the guests at my second grandnephew's baptism, four homeless men. Just after meeting them I was walking up the center aisle of the church with Alexander's hand in mine. Had somebody asked me to describe this empty church in the minute before I led Alexander up to the baptismal font, I would have said, "A typical example of 1950's Catholic church construction. Geometry and utility were in back then, so everything is boxy and straight-edged; lots of dark wood, streaky marble, and terrazzo floors. Even with some of the lights on, the place looked dingy and dull, especially on a typically rainy Northwestern day. The kindest things you could call it were, I guess, anonymous, quiet, and reasonably warm. No wonder the Four Homeless Guys felt comfortable in the portico.

But that was not how it seemed to Alexander. As he looked around, his hand still in mine, he said to me, encouragingly, "It's cute!" No one had probably ever called this ponderous, dark building "cute," but of course that's the word Alexander has probably heard most often in his life as a term of praise, since that's how most people, including perfect strangers taking tolls at the airport parking garage or strolling in the mall, describe *him*.

We went on to baptize Alexander's baby brother, and I tried to involve Alexander in the ceremony as much as I could: he held, very seriously, his brother's unlit baptismal candle, and he tested the water to make sure it was warm enough. Finally we all sang "Jingle Bells," despite the fact that it was almost two months after Christmas. I asked him to start the singing, and that was about the only ritual-oriented song that Alexander knew.

But what stayed with me after the event was Alexander's hopeful vision of the down-at-heels church. I think he was trying to be courteous to me by praising my "home." With his fresh eyes, he also saw beneath the shopworn exterior to the beauty of this House of God, a beauty permanently there because so many people of faith have come inside to meet God. They bring their children there too, just like we had for Alexander's unexpected appraisal and Nicolas's official welcoming.

SIXTEEN

HANK

"Our children are here to stay, but our babies and toddlers and preschoolers are gone as fast as they grow up—and we have only a short moment with each. When you see a grandfather take a baby in his arms, you see that the moment hasn't always been long enough." (St. Clair Adams Sullivan)

Alexander was climbing the wall, again. I stopped rolling the ball to Nicolas and rushed over to grab him. Like the concrete drainage sluice concealed by the tall grass in our backyard, this wall is a magnet for children. There are tiny footholds, which allow small feet to rappel up about five feet and young eyes to peer into the next yard at ground level. It always seems a dangerous endeavor if you're the adult watching that child. Instead of dissuading Alexander from the climb, I have exacted a promise that he will not climb up unless I am there to assist him. I suppose this time he forgot, or perhaps it was this five-year old's declaration of independence, one of several that autumn day.

I ran over ready to grab him about the waist as he neared the top of the wall. Just as he achieve his objective, we simultaneously noticed a monarch butterfly shopping the flowers at our now eye level in the next yard. I ran and grabbed Nicolas and for a few magic seconds the three of us watched and whispered in wonder as we closely observed this beautiful, busy creature. I whispered that it was on its way to winter in a warm place while knowing full well that it would be another generation that would reach that tree in Mexico and not the one we were studying.

For the rest of this visit Nicolas, when in the backyard, would take my hand and urge me in the direction of the patch of flowers just atop the wall. He pulled and grunted until I gathered him in my arms and showed him that the butterfly was gone. He never gave up the hope that it would be there, and I never refused to lift him for the search.

I understood how he felt. We all would like to recapture those unexpected moments when something small becomes large, when an accidental glimpse becomes an indelible memory. I have seen St. Paul's Cathedral, Lake Louise, and the Sydney Bridge, but they do not come close to matching the wonder of that butterfly. I hope that in the future Nicolas will remember the time that he saw a monarch so close that he could study its black veins and white spots as it searched for milkweed among the flowers. I hope that in his trip into the past he will turn and see my face, just as full of the moment as he was.

SEVENTEEN

RUTH

"There are only two lasting bequests we can hope to give our children. One of these is roots; the other, wings." (Hodding Carter)

Our grandsons find our backyard birds fascinating. We have a walkout sliding glass door leading from the kitchen to a patio behind our house. Directly next to it is a large sweet gum tree. Hank always threatens to cut it down because of the prickly gumballs that fall seemingly year round and droppings that bleed on the patio in the spring. However, I always protest loudly. This tree may be a nuisance, but it's the perfect place for a bird feeder. I put out sunflower seeds and suet, and the birds come as soon as I retreat. Our next door neighbors have a birdbath at the edge of their patio. It is quite close to our feeder. Behind our property is a wooded area, a desirable place for wild birds to call home or migrate through.

When Nicolas and Alexander come to visit, they are sure to check several times a day to see if the feeder is full. Alexander likes to climb up the ladder when a refill is needed. He watches out for and chases away the greedy squirrels that tip the feeder to scatter the seeds on the ground to make dining easier. Nicolas will clap when he sees a chipmunk skittering across the patio. Both boys recognize the cardinals immediately and can tell the difference between the male and female. They witness and learn about sparrows, starlings, blue jays, yellow finches, woodpeckers, chickadees, titmice, crows, and robins. A really special occasion finds a hummingbird fluttering among the flowers.

In addition to a pair of binoculars to get a closer look at a bird, the boys share a great book that doesn't overwhelm them. It is *The Big Golden Book of Backyard Birds*. This is a large reference tome with big pictures and text by Kathleen Daly. Illustrations of different types of beaks lead to discussions of foods such as worms, insects, meat, or seeds that birds are able to eat. We look for pictures of the birds at the feeder that are not familiar. We may or may not read the text on the page. Mostly we discuss what the boys are observing. We look at the feet on various types of birds and talk about how they might be used for catching prey or sitting on swaying branches in strong winds. We play the "I see" game. If we take turns, we can keep the game going until the bird flies away.

EIGHTEEN

JIM

"I lift up my eyes to the mountains from whence comes my help." (Psalm 121:1)

Of course I remember the first time I held Alexander. Any grandparent can recall this event. He was ten days old and back from the hospital for a while. I say *for a while* because he was destined to return for gastric reasons. It was October. I held him indoors for a bit, maybe even gave him a bottle. But what was most memorable about this afternoon was that it stopped raining, which is big news in his native Northwest. His mother, seeing the sun penetrate the gloom for the first time in several days, decided to take him for his first outing in his new pram, which was a gift from Stan's mother Marjorie and loaded with extras.

Alexander had several first encounters that day—with the sweet elderly couple next door, with some of the neighborhood kids, even with a "grrr", his word for any dog for several months after he began speaking. He was fascinated with dogs from an early age and eventually paid the price when he stood between a family pet and the pet's food.

But the first encounter I remember best that day was with Mt. St. Helens. It was such an unexpectedly pristine afternoon that you could clearly see what remained of this mountain, which blew off several thousand feet of its top almost fifteen years before Alexander was born. I thought that Alexander

51

ought to know about this unsettling feature of his landscape. I lifted him from the comfortable pram and pointed him toward it, as if he had the ability to both focus on the distant object and understand what I was saying. He actually did begin to cry, although I doubt it was from fear of a rumbling eruption.

For some reason I thought of the scene—is it somewhere in the first episode of Alex Haley's *Roots?*—where someone lifts up the newborn Kunta Kinte to meet sky and wind and stars, the whole of creation. I didn't make that kind of gesture, of course—his mom would have thought I was overstepping priestly bounds. But I thought to myself, as he lay blinking back in his stylish pram, "Alexander, meet the World. World, meet Alexander!"

NINETEEN

HANK

"Our opinion of ourselves, like our shadow, makes us either too big or too little." (Johann Wolfgang von Goethe)

We arrived for Christmas in a festive mood. Lisa and the boys met our plane. Ruth reached down for Nicolas, who was in his stroller. After I hugged Alexander, I stooped too for a hug, and Nicolas cried out, "Jim!"

I was instantly confused and hurt in equal measure. "No, Nic. I'm Grandpa. And I've come to play with you!" I added like a game show host. I hugged him anyway.

"Jim!" he reiterated. "Jim!"

My campaign to gain identity began. We went to the top level of the parking lot to watch planes take off and land. "Papa!" Nicolas shouted as he pointed skyward.

"Yes, Papa," I explained. "He flies a plane. And I'm Grandpa. I write about you. Me. Grandpa."

"Jim," Nicolas said as he nodded sagely in agreement, apparently sorry about my confusion.

I don't think we are much alike in appearance or personality. Jim and I. I'm virtually hairless, while Jim has been able to hold on to curly locks. Our facial features wouldn't necessarily announce brotherhood. I am a bit more diverse in interests, but Jim is more intelligent. I am tiresomely neat. I could go on, but I think you get the point. The one thing we both have in abundance is a patient, inexhaustible capacity to play with the boys. So it is somewhat natural, I suppose, that they respond to us somewhat equally.

But I do puzzles, swim, build with Legos, and skip. Jim, less physical, excels in dinosaur dialogue and other fantasy play. So our activities are different. And I would think that Nicolas would recognize the differences between us.

No. For seven days I was Jim no matter how often I explained, borderline irked, that I was *NOT* Jim.

Mid week I began to anticipate what Nicolas would do when the real Jim showed up on the day after Christmas. Would he point to me, yell "Imposter!" and fling himself into Jim's arms to be carried away without looking back? Would he chuckle and say, "Grandpa," as he reddened in embarrassment and I assured him with a hug that I was not hurt.

Although I was. Hurt because Jim gets to see him more often. Hurt because if Jim were the priority name in Nicolas's consciousness, he was probably the priority figure. Hurt because my importance seemed diminished in what I thought was my most important role at this stage of my life. Identity, or how we perceive ourselves and are perceived by others, no matter the age, is all.

When Jim came through the door, I went over to stand beside him. I said to Nicolas, who was nearby at the game table, "See. This is Jim, and I'm Grandpa." I grinned winningly as if participating in a Mr. Senior America contest.

Nicolas looked at me. He blinked. He looked at Jim and blinked. "Come on, play, Jim," he said as he ran over and pulled Jim's hand toward the fun.

Did he, could he, see the difference? I'm not sure. He is not yet two years old. Did it still matter? Not in the least. Over time, I suppose, I became used to being called Jim and I began to realize that it was a compliment. Jim is his favorite visitor; and if I am confused with him, that just means that I am his equal, if not separate. And, anyway, love does not exist in compartments. Nicolas, who has recently decided that my name is Paca, won't love me less because he has a loving uncle. He will love me more.

TWENTY

RUTH

"No matter what accomplishments you make, somebody helps you." (Althea Gibson Darben)

Alexander calls his father *Papa*. Like many children, Alexander thinks Papa can do everything. One summer Stan put together quite a large redwood structure in the backyard that requires yearly maintenance. It houses a slide, swings, a fort, a tire swing, climbing bars, a driving wheel, and a telescope for imaginative play. Inside the house, in a large, unfurnished room, he constructed a huge play table at a small child's level that has a multitude of uses.

Everyone in the family benefits from Stan's hard work, especially his sons. Alexander uses every opportunity to get one of his grandparents to spend time at either or both play stations. I especially like to play outside on the swings and in the fort. Alexander pretends he's a pirate, a pilot, a captain at sea, a bus driver, or a fireman. Sometimes the Rainbow, the structure's actual name, changes in a flash from a ladder against a burning building into a control tower, where we are watching for planes. The pretend, *theme for the day* play usually has a beginning, middle, and end. Alexander likes to assign my role. Sometime I fly a plane because, "There *are* lady pilots," he informs me with great seriousness. Sometimes I am to watch for other ships on a dangerous sea. My absolute favorite is playing firefighter because we go down the slide to get to the truck as fast as we can. Whatever the story might be, there is always lots of excitement and quick action. None of it would be possible without Stan's efforts.

Eric Carle knows well the power that children feel their fathers possess. He addresses this in his story *Papa, Please Get the Moon for Me*. On the first page Monica wants to play with the moon but can't reach it. She asks her father to get it for her. Papa gets a long ladder and goes to a very high mountain. When he stretches the ladder from the mountain to the moon, the page folds out to dramatically show the length of the ladder and the distance he needs to climb for his daughter. Papa finds the moon is too large for Monica to play with, but he knows that it will get smaller in time. He climbs down and Monica jumps and dances while hugging the moon, which continues to get smaller and smaller each night. It finally disappears completely. Soon a thin white sliver of the moon reappears. It grows and glows until we see it full again.

Loving adults like Stan are interested in giving to the next generation. To help his children not just grow but to thrive, he expends a lot of energy and spends a lot of leisure time making sure his sons will have focused activities and the equipment for playtime. This attention to manuals, put-together instructions, and mundane maintenance helps their imaginations to develop.

TWENTY-ONE

JIM

God says, "I have called you by your name—you are mine."
(Isaiah 43:1)

Grandchildren often call us by special names, especially if they have a whole set of four grandparents that they need to keep straight. Sometimes these names get chosen when the grandchildren garble our real names or the word for "grandfather" or "grandmother" in English, Spanish, Japanese, French, Italian, Yiddish, and so on. But once they have called us by our names, we grow into them. We become them. And no one else on earth has that name. It's like getting a job description; it's like finding out, finally, what you were put on earth to do. It's validating, assuring, and altogether wonderful.

When Alexander was three, he went through a phase where he was working on job titles. He would go up to perfect strangers and tell them, with appropriate gestures, "This is my maman. . . . This is my papa." Around that time he and I went to the zoo; we were checking out the polar bears in their climate controlled habitat when a pretty little girl came up to the next window with her family. Alexander glanced over, and with a fine nonchalance, airily waved at me and said, "This is my Jim."

I'm glad to be a great-uncle since I get to find out, every time I'm with my grand-nephews, what being a Jim entails. I like to think of Jims as being rather like the genie in Aladdin—fun in a wacky kind of way and with remarkable powers to make wishes come true, within certain limits. This would, of course, not be the Jim that their parents would know. I hope that their Jim is dependable and caring. In any event, I don't think I was ever a full-fledged Jim until Alexander dubbed me.

TWENTY-TWO

HANK

"Do not judge others, and God will not judge you, do not condemn others, and God will not condemn you; forgive others, and God will forgive you. Give to others, and God will give to you." (Luke 6.37)

My grandsons are lucky, and so are Ruth and I. They have four actively involved but very different grandparents endlessly promoting their welfare, and we have made two special friends. When we are all together, three generations, the number one activity on everyone's agenda is to have fun and celebrate our family.

Among the four of us, the older generation, we have most bases covered. Marjorie, or Grandmere, has highly evolved social skills. She is competent in the completion of any domestic undertaking whether it's to repair a rip in a shirt or to prepare a formal, very elegant dinner for twelve. She is charming, laughs easily, and she's a good listener. Jean Claude, or Grandpere, has a business mind. It has helped him make several fortunes in his sixty years. He has guts but balances risk with intuition. Since his days in the French navy, he has always been a citizen of the world; and he will make sure that his grandsons learn to sail a boat, negotiate a deal, and explore places where few have been before.

Ruth and I, Grandpa and Grandma, used to worry about what would happen should there be offspring in the international, culturally diffuse marriage that our daughter had entered into. Her in-laws seemed to have been everywhere and done everything. They spoke of friends and acquaintances all over the world, and they had the resources to visit them often.

But we found our strengths. Our grandsons will always love to learn because Grandma is a master teacher who organizes stimulating projects and then has several books to read, which tie everything together, promote further thinking, and prepare their young minds for the next opportunity to learn. Because of me they will know the arts and love to read.

That so many personalities and backgrounds can come to the table and enjoy the same meal is a source of both wonder and relief. It ensures that the next generation will never know boredom (except in the angst filled and ennui driven teen years). Alexander and Nicolas will be more complete men because of the differences that the four of us have brought to our relationships with them. As luck would have it, the quality that makes us similar is the ability to share.

I should have remembered that in this life most anticipated fears are either unfounded or reasonably easy to head off. It's the hidden cord, the black ice, and the sudden pain in the chest that you have to worry about.

TWENTY-THREE

Ruth

"The supreme happiness of life is the conviction that we are loved." (Victor Hugo)

According to Justin Kaplan in his book *The Language of Names*, "...names penetrate the core of our being and are a form of poetry, storytelling, magic and compressed history." I agree.

When our daughter Lisa was pregnant with a second child, the search for the best choice began. She would check out various names with me over the phone. Having dealt with hundreds of children's names in classrooms over many years and having seen the impact that his or her name has on the child's daily life, I emphasized the importance of giving my grandchild a strong name. Stan, our son-in-law, wanted to make sure that the final choice included his heritage. After many long deliberations they decided on Nicolas Louis James. Spelling it *Nicolas* honored his French heritage, and Louis was in memory of Stan's mother's father. James represented the influence of one of the writers of this book. To me, these were wise choices.

Bill Martin's book *Knots on a Counting Rope* speaks to the importance of a strong name. The blind boy in the story wants his grandfather to tell him who he is. The grandfather ties a knot in the rope, which represents the passage of time, and with each knot he tells the grandson about the importance of his name. "When the rope is filled with knots, you will know the story by heart and can tell it to yourself," the grandfather instructs the boy, who gains confidence from the story of his own name.

As the years roll forward there will be many family stories to share with Nicolas about each person his name represents. We hope that these tales will make him stronger and that he will never feel alone. When the grandfather says, "My love will always surround you," Bill Martin reminds us of what ties the generations together in addition to our names.

TWENTY-FOUR

JIM

"Peace I leave with you; peace is my gift to you." (John 14: 27)

For some years now, since the Second Vatican Council (1962-65), it has been the custom at the Catholic Mass to shake hands just before the Communion part of the service, during which people share bread and wine. This was an ancient part of the ritual, the Greeting of Peace, but over the centuries, as often happens, it had become stylized and finally restricted to the celebrating clergy, whose backs were otherwise to the congregation for most of the mass. They formally bowed to each other and said, in Latin, "Peace be with you." Unless you were a liturgy student or knew Latin, you wouldn't have known what was going on up there on that little private island.

After Vatican II, the custom was revived and brought up to date. All words were now in English, everybody got to join in, and a handshake was suggested as an equivalent gesture of peaceableness. Historically, in fact, shaking hands was a way of showing that you didn't have a ready weapon. At first, many Catholics (except for the extroverts) were acutely uncomfortable with this action: it meant having to communicate with, and to touch, complete strangers. Of course the whole idea was that, if we're praying together, we ought to be at peace, and we ought not to be strangers. Over the years the gesture has caught on; and, if anything, things have gone to the other extreme. People run about exchanging exuberant greetings, even hugs and kisses, with lots and lots of people. Sometimes, when I watch the resulting melee, I'm reminded of the custom that Native American warriors called "counting coups," because the peace-exchangers seem to be attempting to touch as many people as they can. When I officiate at mass, it's sometimes hard to settle people down again so that Communion can go forward.

Even people who don't much like the Greeting of Peace would have gotten into it, though, if they'd been at a Mass I attended with Alexander and his parents when he was about three. Actually he'd been in and out of the church that day, as his attention came and went. There weren't many distracting pictures in the hymnbooks, so during the homily I took him outside to inspect the shrubbery. We came back inside shortly before the Greeting and climbed into the pew with his parents. Alexander immediately decided that he wanted to join in. After hugging me and his mom and dad, he motioned toward a woman nearby. Touching just her did not satisfy him. He was still small enough to be carried, so I took him from person to person. Alexander would look each stranger in the eye, smile charmingly, and whisper, "Pea." Everybody he brought "Pea" to smiled back. God's peace reached every one of them, I would like to believe.

TWENTY-FIVE

Hank

"All genuine knowledge originates in direct experience."
(Mao Tse-tung)

Alexander told me on the phone that this Halloween he will dress as Superman. Well, I *am* Superman.

Our community opened a new pool. It was a marvel of size and imagination, with spouting fountains and sliding ramps, and totally kid friendly. I could hardly wait to take Alexander, who was just beginning to feel comfortable in the water. He would attempt swimming strokes if he knew that the bottom of the pool was easily attainable, but he resisted efforts to get him to float on his back. He wanted to be left alone if the water was only up to his waist, but he wanted to cling to me if it came up to his shoulders.

I observed from a slight distance as he came sliding down a tube into two feet of water. Apprehension was on his face as he plummeted. But he did it again with greater confidence. I watched as he attempted to join two boys who were engaged in the same activity. After the third descent together, they chased Alexander, grabbed him, and pushed his head under the water. It was somewhat playful so I did nothing. This was, I told myself, not life threatening, and I wanted to see how Alexander handled the situation. Then they did it again and I edged closer. Laughing uproariously, they released him. Alexander was not frightened, but he moved away, went to the larger pool, and waded in. A few minutes later, the slightly older of the two boys came over and pushed him under again, and the other held his head under the water a longer time. This time it was vicious. I waded over, grabbed their arms, and told them to desist or face dire consequences. They moved away, eyeing me over their shoulders, and went to tell their parents, who didn't react other than to shrug their shoulders. They were too busy with their tans to care.

Relieved that I would not face a charge of assault or child molestation, or both, I told Alexander that there are both good boys and bad boys in this world. The ones who ganged up on him in evil delight were bad ones.

Over the next few days he repeated the incident and my words to everyone who would listen. He asked me repeatedly to retell the story about the bad boys at the pool and how I rescued him. In the eyes of my grandson, I was, at least for a few days, a comic book hero. Although it was a nice feeling, I worried that I had interfered in a situation that, had I waited a bit longer, might have taught Alexander a lesson in how to handle bullies.

By playing Superman, did I deny him the chance, later on, to become a super man?

TWENTY-SIX

RUTH

"The Lord has given us eyes to see with and ears to listen with." (Proverbs 20.12)

We live in Missouri, a state with many caves. The next time Alexander visits, we will take him cave exploring because now that he is moving beyond childhood he has an interest. It began last year when we were in Florida with him and Hurricane Irene blew through. We had lots of time for flashlight reading during the power outages. Since bats are the only flying mammal and Alexander knows that he is a mammal too, reading *Stellaluna* stimulated his interest in caves as we discussed where bats live. In this charming book Janell Cannon tells a story about a tiny fruit bat. One night Mother Bat was flying and carrying her baby Stellaluna when a powerful owl struck them in mid air. Stellaluna fell to the forest below but survived and joined three baby birds in their nest. She began to learn to eat and sleep differently. After a flying lesson, she found herself on a tree branch with a colony of bats. After much questioning, she learned that one of them was her lost mother. Order was restored when Stellaluna discovered that she could eat fruit instead of yucky bugs, hang upside down, and fly at night while exploring her night vision. Alexander and I talked about the special ability of bats to use echolocation, using their ears to navigate. He was fascinated.

We had thought that we would play on the beach together, but the hurricane made that impossible. Luckily, I had brought the game of Stellaluna along with the book to entertain us at night. Without even a slight exaggeration, I would venture to say that we played it twenty times each day. Alexander loved to turn over the disks and say, "I've got Night Vision!" or "Mother Bat," with great authority. He never wanted to place the Great Owl on the board, fearing that one of us would have to jump back three spaces if we turned it over. God forbid!

A few weeks later Alexander was playing the same game with Grandmere Marjorie. Alexander was supplying a running dialogue about all the things he knew about bats when she said, "You know, in New Caledonia, where my sister lives, people eat bats." Alexander was beside himself with shock. After a pause in the action he replied, "I'm going to tell my teacher." His preschool teacher, you see, is his prime educational authority figure. He just knew that the esteemed Mrs. Reeves would really appreciate, and be grossed out by, his new knowledge.

As a classroom teacher myself, I am touched by the value Alexander is beginning to place upon both learning and the sharing of ideas.

TWENTY-SEVEN

JIM

"Suddenly I meet your face" (Yeats, "A Deep-Sworn Vow")

I'm not having a very good day as I write this. It's a Monday in Seattle, and there are few grayer, colder realities. I'm not certain what's going on, but I sometimes think that some of the people I work with are even crazier than I am. At a committee meeting the other day, a colleague of mine pitched a fit to the point that she sounded like Frau Blucher in *Young Frankenstein*. My ears are still ringing.

At times like this, I do *on purpose* something I learned *by accident* some time ago. I think of the boys. I remember that, the last time I saw Alexander, he ran up to my car when I arrived and shouted, "I *like* you!" I remember how Nicolas chortled when I bounced him down the stairs on my knee. And of course I have to smile, and my day brightens.

People do lots of things to improve their mood. Some of those things, like psychoactive chemicals, work fairly well at first but have bad side effects and stop working over time. Other mood improvers, like exercise, take a certain amount of discipline and preparation, requirements which harried humans may not feel like summoning at that moment. But grandchildren are the best mood-elevators yet devised. They never stop working like drugs and alcohol do as their effects on the brain and nervous system fade. The immediate side effects—a rush of generosity and good humor—are excellent. As St. Paul dryly says, "Against such things there is no law." And finally, I can think of them any where and any when, even though we're separated by time and distance. All these qualities suggest a point I've made elsewhere. Grandchildren bring us very close to God. We only become addicted to inadequate substitutes. For me, God is whatever is so full of love that I can never become addicted to it, because it never fails to satisfy. To remember grandchildren is not just a mood alterer; it is also, and by its nature, a prayer.

TWENTY-EIGHT

Hank

"A woman's guess is much more accurate than a man's certainty." (Rudyard Kipling)

On a shelf in our den is a small marble bust of Nefertiti. Ruth's mother Thelma brought it back from Egypt many years ago. Next to it is an impractical but lovely Japanese vase depicting golden-winged cranes in flight against a blue sky. We bought it in Chicago in a Japanese mall. On a reflective surface that makes it appear to be gliding through deep water rests a hand-carved wooden sailboat that we bought in Finland last summer. Just behind these treasures is a ceramic tile containing one Alexander handprint. Guess which of these is my favorite?

Every time Alexander comes to visit, he insists that we get down this artifact, which is dated December 1997, so that he can place his hand directly over the print. It has become both his own personal measure of his own growth and a means to demonstrate to us how big he is becoming. Next we go into the kitchen-art gallery and admire his latest drawings on the refrigerator.

In a box downstairs is a cardboard and aluminum foil Christmas tree ornament that Lisa made for us when she was a little girl. It is not only a priceless treasure but it is also a symbol of family continuity. As our children were growing up, Ruth insisted each year that they make their own Christmas gifts. Such a project would never have occurred to me, but I now see its value in passing on the true meaning of gift giving. Lisa continues the tradition, so now Alexander's ceramic handprint rests not too far from a plaster hamburger with painstakingly painted sesame seeds on top that his Uncle Matt made in 1980, when he was ten.

When Alexander arrived for his most recent visit, he came running toward me from the top of the passenger ramp clutching a piece of paper. "This is for you, Grandpa!" he said, almost too excited to hug me back.

I studied the drawing and could tell that it was a building of some type. Knowing that a current passion was knights and dragons, I correctly surmised that before me was a medieval fortress. "What a castle!" I exclaimed.

Alexander beamed. "That's the alligator in the water in the front," he said pointing to it but being careful not to get his finger too near to the gaping mouth and teeth.

"The moat," I instructed.

"That's the tower where they watch for bad people," he continued.

"They called them turrets," I said. Turning it this way and that, I added, "I love it, Alexander," And I do. It's in the box with Lisa's ornament.

Christmas is next month. Nicolas is almost two. I wonder what he'll be making for us?

TWENTY-NINE

Ruth

"Anything you're good at contributes to happiness."
(Bertrand Russell)

Let's see. So far this visit we have gone on a one day trip to a farm, been to OMSI, the Oregon Museum of Science and Industry, for a discovery day, watched special videos, played in the backyard with the neighborhood children, and read lots of books. Today it's raining, not unusual for the Northwest, and the thought of going out is not appealing. As I watch Alexander and Nicolas eat breakfast, I am thinking that it is the perfect day for a simple indoor activity. I have just the books to help.

Over and over again, a series of preschool activities by Linda Allison and Martha Weston have come to my rescue. Even though they were written specifically for preschool children and are age appropriate, I find that some of the activities are great for older children as well. They are kid friendly projects that do not require a large amount of preparation. *Wordsaroni, Razzle Dazzle Doodle Art, Pint-Size Science, and Eenie Meenie Miney Math* are the titles.

This particular day I chose the "cool jewels" idea from *Eenie Meenie*. After scanning the pantry for pasta with a wide hole in the center, I mixed food coloring and rubbing alcohol together in small jars and added three types of pasta shapes for a few minutes. After they dried, the boys and I started

SECOND HELPINGS

stringing necklaces. At first I began a color pattern of red and blue pasta beads for Alexander to follow; but he wanted to create his own pattern. He worked until all the pasta shells were strung, and he proudly gave everyone in the household his or her very own piece of jewelry. Nicolas stayed with the activity to its conclusion, and when I put the necklace he had made around his neck and showed him how he looked in the mirror, he grinned with pleasure but then yanked it off. Each of the finished necklaces was beautiful and unique. It turned out to be just the type of project that makes kids especially happy and involved.

The *Razzle Dazzle Doodle Art* book has projects that will help your grandchild boost his/her self-esteem, and they are also a great way to teach cooperation. *Wordsaroni* encourages playing with language by introducing concept words like *behind* and *beside* to, say, a three-year old, who routinely knows three to six hundred words. This is the ideal time during the development of language skills for playing with words and rhymes. *Pint-size Science* helps a child discover the world by using simple things around the house such as magnets or soap bubbles to experiment in open-ended play labs.

All of the challenges that these books offer to preschool children help them problem solve, and they foster skills at a very early age that he and she can use later. They will also help you survive a rainy morning that seems twelve hours long.

THIRTY

JIM

"I thank you for the wonder of my being, for the wonders of all your creation." (Psalm 139:14)

Alexander has always liked to—as the British say—"potter." And his baby brother is exhibiting the same trait. Alexander could amuse himself in the most barren environment imaginable, picking up whatever twigs and rocks and bits of string were available and staring at them fascinated. While watching him, I had to be more than usually observant to prevent him from examining, and perhaps tasting, discarded cigarette butts, used Band-Aids, and the like. Maybe because their papa is an engineer, both boys are just as enthralled by gadgets as they are by natural objects. They cannot pass by tools, switches, fire extinguishers, and, like all other children, drinking fountains, without examining them.

One evening I was out to a restaurant with Alexander, his dad, and a pilot friend of his dad's. Since dad and friend wanted to talk shop, Alexander and I went outside. All there was to see or examine around Red Robin was some perfunctory landscaping—bits of bark, hardy plants, layers of rock, concrete edging. But we weren't bored for a minute while looking at and feeling the differences between one piece of bark and another or one oval gray rock and another. I was too big for this activity, but Alexander was just the right size to walk down the elevated concrete strip, all the time pushing my hands away except when it was time to jump into my arms. We barely had time to notice the cars and vans and trucks that kept coming into and going out of the busy restaurant's parking lot.

I notice that now that Alexander is older, he focuses on toys more and on humble bits of creation less. But I'll remember how fresh it all seemed to him, and newly of interest to me, when he brought what Zen practitioners call Beginner's Mind to the unobtrusive pleasures of this world.

Thirty-One

Hank

"The quickest way for a parent to get a child's attention is to sit down and look comfortable." (Lane Olinghouse)

    I suspect it's partially my age, but I have the daily newspaper habit. Neither of my children nor any of their friends do because there is TV, and the Net, and the daily responsibilities. While visiting, I am in the habit of going after The Oregonian each morning and the New York Times on Sunday. As I read, at some point Alexander will sneak up and hit the newspaper from behind causing me to shout and complain. The little devil has the uncanny ability to know just when I am engrossed enough in a story to let down my guard. Now used to the game, I oftentimes anticipate his approach and put the paper down just before impact. I glare at him disapprovingly causing much head bobbing and gales of laughter, on his part.
    If anyone but him did this, I would be offended. But for us it has become a game, a habit that binds us to each other. He is not trying to get my attention or make me angry. He wants to see if he can get away with one more stealthy approach and win a round. I want to spy his furtive rounding of the coffee table on his knees and announce triumphantly that I'm on to him.
    In all great and lasting relationships there are rituals that mean something only to the participants. I will be sad on the day when he allows me to read my newspaper without interruption, but I don't expect that any time soon.

THIRTY-TWO

RUTH

"The hardest job kids face today is learning good manners without seeing any." (Fred Astaire)

In Stan and Lisa's house meals are shared as a family, a common French, definitely not American, custom. The table is set, napkins are used on a regular basis, and everyone in the house must assemble for meals. The boys have routinely been taught table manners. Alexander must not rush to get down from his chair. He must wait until the adults are done and then ask permission to leave the table. Hands are washed before and after each meal. All the common courtesy words, like *merci* or thank you, are reinforced. When company comes to visit, mealtime becomes a *very* special event. Serving in the French style, the presentation of food becomes even more important; and each course is served in a particular order beginning with sausages or other meats and ending with salad before dessert.

Being with early primary children in a school setting nine months of the year, I see many children who eat using few manners and have little respect for other common courtesies. I assume that these children have not acquired table manners either because their parents do not value them or have failed to reinforce them. I sometimes wonder if Alexander will continue to be mannerly when he spends more and more time at school, peer pressure prevails, and appearances (to fit in) become so important.

Mind Your Manners, Ben Bunny is a lift-the-flap book about table manners. In this short rhyming book Mavis Smith works on the key words and practices that children should have exposure to on a daily basis. They are using a napkin, removing a cap, staying in your chair, not playing with your food, taking small bites, saying *thank you* and *excuse me*, and chewing the food properly with your mouth closed. How to phrase a question like, "Would you please be kind enough to pass the cheese?" or "May I please be excused?" are included. Cute animal characters such as a rabbit, a dog, and a crow enhance meaningful text.

We know how important it is to be consistent; so when Alexander comes to visit us, we use the basic table rules that are practiced at home but do not necessarily serve in the French style. Alexander, like so many other children, must get used to living in two or more cultures.

THIRTY-THREE

JIM

"Be happy at all times; pray constantly; and for all things give thanks to God." (First Thessalonians 5:17-18)

One of Alexander's nicer features is the courteous way he treats gifts. I'm far from impartial when it comes to Alexander, of course, but still I think this is somewhat unusual. I don't think I was like this as a kid. I've been in situations where children don't say *Thank you* for a gift, or have had to be prompted, mechanically, with, "What do you say....?" But he seems genuinely thrilled by each and every gift he gets. One Christmas he received a very advanced electronic fire engine from one set of grandparents—so elaborate, in fact, that for the next Christmas he asked for a more mundane fire engine so that he and his friends could have something less complex to play with. It's not that he didn't like it. He asked for and received lessons in how to make the grand fire engine do all of its tricks—raising and lowering ladders, blowing its siren, flashing its lights. But I remember he was just as excited about my far more humble gift: I got him a box full of road construction toys and another set, a fairly complete collection of airport toys—planes and trucks and forklifts. I told him that if he mixed the two sets together he would pretty much have his local airport, which has been under reconstruction for what seems like decades. Again, he couldn't wait to get every single plastic piece out of both boxes and onto the rug, where the mingled sets made an impressive miniature display.

What is perhaps even more remarkable, though, is what happened after the initial excitement of opening these gifts. The cliché is that kids will open presents and then neglect items, like the Ultimate Fire Extinguisher, in favor of playing with the box it came in. But not my Alexander. Over the hours and days after Christmas morning gift opening, he spent some time with each and every present, even-handed in his delight in all of them. Eventually, of course, all of the toys got mixed together in an epic tale of childish fantasy that all childen create as their imaginations expand. That's as it should be. No present, especially our God-gifted imagination, should be ignored or slighted. If neglected, it fizzes out, like the fire on the receiving end of the Ultimate Fire Engine's performance.

It seems to me that this is the way we should be with all the gifts we get, from people or from God. A friend once gave me an audiotape of some religious songs that she liked; I went into paroxysms of self-abasement, saying it was too much, I already had plenty of tapes, I only listen to classical music, etc. Finally, amused and exasperated, she said, "Jim—just say thank you." And so I did. And so, without prompting, does Alexander. Giving a present is a generous act, receiving it is an art.

THIRTY-FOUR

HANK

"Success isn't permanent, and failure isn't fatal." (Mike Ditka)

Alexander was a difficult baby at times. We saw him only sporadically during his first few years, so I did not witness the occasional incidents that his parents called meltdowns. Reportedly, he would tense up, scream uncontrollably, and resist all efforts to comfort him. I thought that they were exaggerating when describing this behavior.

Ruth, Lisa, and I went to a Hannah Anderson children's clothing sale so big that it was held in the Convention Center. I offered to entertain Alexander, who was two months shy of his second birthday, while the ladies concentrated on the great bargains. Lisa handed him over with no hesitation, and I was both proud that she trusted me and certain that he and I would have a great time. The ladies disappeared into a phalanx of women with armfuls of outfits.

Alexander grunted and pointed toward the tables heaped with clothing, and I knew that he wanted to follow his Mother. This, of course, was natural in a two-year old. "No, Alexander. Momma's busy, and we're going to have some fun," I said, bouncing him on my arm. "Let's start with a treat!"

He was not convinced, and the grunts became more distressed as I walked toward the food concessions. Realizing that this was the opposite direction to his will, and his Mother, Alexander tried to get down.

"Let's get a cookie," I suggested brightly as he squirmed in my arms and fought for his freedom. We joined the line, and I noticed mostly sympathetic stares and received a number of offers to help.

There were no cookies, but I somehow managed to grab a muffin and a drink and pay for it. Alexander wouldn't stop screaming long enough to try the muffin, and he swatted the orange juice away with the back of his hand. It, of course, ended up on the table and floor. He next reactivated his campaign to be let down so that he might find someone who could understand his needs. I accepted defeat. "Let's go find Momma," I suggested, and his sobs became a bit less frantic. I headed into the shoppers, could not spot Lisa, and retreated toward the door. On the sidewalk, I began talking about cars, birds, the sun, and slowly the storm clouds lifted and calm was restored. To this day I do not understand why being outside changed his mood.

Twenty minutes later, Lisa came out and said, "Oh, there you are! We wondered if something happened."

"Not a thing," I said breezily as we piled into the car.

I was extremely glad that Alexander was too young to talk for he would surely have told his mother that I was a totally unsuitable caretaker. I now had new knowledge. Mommy fixation can not be denied as long as her ions are in the air, and meltdowns were not exaggerated. I prayed that I would never witness another, but sometimes our prayers are not answered.

THIRTY-FIVE

RUTH

"A person's words can be a source of wisdom, deep as the ocean, fresh as a flowing stream." (Proverbs 18.4)

There is always that time when children become naturally curious about all those symbols (adults call them words) on billboards and packages and in books. This curiosity comes during no certain developmental stage and depends on the individual child, but this is where the real work of language instruction starts. English is an overwhelming set of symbols for the beginner to conquer because it borrows from many, many sources and there are usually exceptions to each of its language rules. Alexander and Nicolas have an additional challenge. They must be fluent in two languages to communicate with the family abroad.

Opportunities for success in learning both English and French have become a welcomed responsibility for both sets of grandparents. When the boys and I are riding in the car, we take delight in playing a game of, "Can you find a D?" All the passengers are busily checking out the signs, license plates, and trucks to be the first to answer. The winner gets to call the next letter or number to look for. When we are reading a book, I run my fingers over the words to set the left to right progression; and the boys know a period means stop because my finger does. We review the order of letters to make sure they are in their right places when Alexander signs his name. These routine activities heighten awareness of the sight and sounds of each letter.

The French grandparents are interested in both correct pronunciation and communication because these are such important aspects of their culture. French is an especially beautiful language to hear, and everyone who has had dinner with a French family knows how the conversation flows. Jean Claude and Marjorie always speak French to the boys, and both Alexander and Nicolas understand them because Stan, our son-in-law, consistently uses it in the home when speaking to his sons. Sometimes Alexander will mix the two languages in a sentence, a natural way for him to express himself at age five. At the age of two, Nicolas carries on complete conversations in French with Grandmere Marjorie, and she beams with pleasure.

As children move from spoken words to the written text, using a rebus book makes the job of learning easier and less threatening. Rebus writing use pictures in the place of some words to tell a story. As the reader approaches the picture words, the listener waits in anticipation for his or her part, calling the name of the object at the appropriate time. Two books that are especially fun are *The Jacket I Wear in the Snow* by Shirley Neitzel and *Bug in a Rug Reading Fun For Just-Beginners* by Joanna Cole, which has different activities on each page. A few pages even introduce the very young to diagram reading, words and arrows, which point to objects as they identify parts of the body, items in a bedroom, and so on.

THIRTY-SIX

JIM

"Your majesty is praised above the heavens, on the lips of children and of babies." (Psalm 8: 1-2)

Nicolas, nearly two, is developing language, and I'm as fascinated as I was when Alexander went through it. This is the phase when he picks up lots of English, and lots of French too. I remember Alexander shouting, "Regarde!" ("Look!") to his French grandmother at about this age, which delighted both she and me. But what's more interesting than the process is that children don't necessarily wait to master adult language before they use words. They create their own language and are fluent in it.

One of Alexander's favorite pastimes at this age was to take me into the unfinished attic of his parents' house. There he would grab a plastic wand that was part of an unused playpen and start pointing and gesticulating at different features of the attic, chattering away unintelligibly to me, for all the world like a two-year-old real estate pitchman. He called my attention to joists and insulation, and he had names for them.

Nicolas also has his own language these days. I can even do some comparative linguistics between the two brothers. For some reason, I assumed they might use the same made-up words for the same things, but it doesn't work that way. Given Nicolas's stout sense of independence from his brother, I suppose it's no wonder that he would insist on his own words.

Indeed, it's a very good thing that I've noted that Nicolasian is quite different from Alexandrian, because otherwise there could have been a contretemps. Alexander used "B" or perhaps "Bee" to denote a mess in his diapers, as in the fateful phrase, "Have you got a bee, Alexander?" I didn't really want to know the answer when I was baby-sitting him alone by the way. But for Nicolas, "Bee" means airplane, and the idea is inextricably bound up with "Papa," who flies "Bees." A gentle reminder, this, that for every new child it's a completely new world which requires its own language.

THIRTY-SEVEN

HANK

"Give God time." (The Koran)

Between the ages of two and three, Alexander developed a taste for vanilla shakes. Every time we would stop for one, he would position the straw in the center of his mouth and, head bowed, he would ingest the cold sweetness slowly. It was a serious enterprise.

After a decent interval I would always ask, "Alexander, may I have a taste of your shake?"

Without a pause for air or a glimmer of hesitation, he would slowly shake his head back and forth, not up and down. I was not to share. Two-year olds are notoriously selfish. I didn't lecture, didn't insist. I didn't even sigh.

Last spring I took Alexander to a class about mammal babies at Powder Valley, a woodsy park with fine children's programs. We saw mother possums, foxes, and robins, and their adorable offspring as we listened about their habits and behaviors. We took several trails into the woods and studied trees and rocks.

I don't know if there was a relationship between these events, but on the way home Alexander asked if we could stop and pick up a birthday cake for his Mom. The bakery offered a free cookie to all small children, and I wondered if this was the true motive, but I didn't probe. Any generous impulse is progress. He did not take much time to select the cake. It was chocolate, her favorite. We paid for this cake, and I treated him to a shake.

After a decent interval I asked, "Alexander, may I taste your shake?"

The head predictably moved back and forth.

Alexander was four when we visited in July. I pulled him and his brother in a wagon down to the vacant lot where wild flowers grew in abundance. "Stop!" he said. "I want to pick some flowers for my Mom."

After a stern lecture about *not* picking cultivated flowers that *belong* to property owners and *not* picking flowers in parks and in other places where environmental sensitivity is required, I allowed him to harvest a few wild daisies and bluebells. Clutching his bouquet, he climbed back into the wagon, we hurried home, and he handed them to his mother, who thanked him and repeated my lecture.

Picking flowers had been hot, thirsty work, so I suggested, "Why don't we go for a vanilla shake?" It was a popular idea.

In the car at Burgerville, I waited until Alexander was deeply into his shake before I asked. "Alexander, may I have a taste?"

"Sure," he said without hesitation, and he thrust the cup toward me.

Surprised and pleased, I pretended to slurp and returned it with a thank you.

I remembered this today when the Police Benevolent Society called and asked me to help with the scholarship fund for the sons and daughters of officers killed in the line of duty.

"Sure," I said and made a donation.

Sharing has its time.

THIRTY-EIGHT

RUTH

"Loving a child doesn't mean giving in to all his whims to love him is to bring out the best in him, to teach him to love what is difficult." (Nadia Boulanger)

Lisa and I usually spend some time on the phone each night. It may be only a two-minute conversation. The real purpose of the call is to be assured that everyone in both households is O.K. Usually, when Stan is flying, I can hear the grandsons in the background because they are never too far from Lisa's side when he is away. Many evenings they will interrupt her to show something they are making, or Alexander will ask to talk on the phone with grandma or grandpa. Recently Nicolas found a hole in Lisa's sock, stuck his finger inside, and tickled her toe. As she laughed in my ear, he, enjoying his mother's delight, repeated the action. It was so immediate that I felt tickled too.

Generally mothers, who usually spend more time with the children than any other adult, are left with the primary responsibility of creating a happy and nurturing home environment. Lisa provides a warm, loving space for our grandsons. There is a two-hour time difference between our homes, and on many occasions I speak with Lisa after our evening meal but before theirs. Alexander is often helping his mom prepare dinner. He loves to mix batter or push the toast down in the toaster. Whenever Alexander and I organize a project, he always insists that the first of whatever we make be for his mom. In the book *Real Boys* by William Pollack, he says, "The love of a mother, in most cases, is what will help a boy launch himself into a healthy masculine life."

Martin Waddell wrote a sensitive book entitled *Good Job, Little Bear* for children beginning to explore the world beyond their immediate home. Little Bear leads the way. He wants Big Bear to watch him learn to scale a rock, climb a tree, or jump into the stream. In each case Little Bear knows instinctively that Big Bear supports him. Big Bear reassures Little Bear with each new adventure by repeating the words, "Good job, Little Bear. I'll be there when you need me always."

Our grandsons sense they will always be able to depend on Lisa to be there for them. Her love makes our grandsons emotionally and psychologically strong. What a mom. What a blessing!

THIRTY-NINE

JIM

"See, I make all things new." (Revelations 21:5)

Nicolas is seventeen months old, and he can still be lifted easily (Alexander weighs fifty pounds and can't, at least by me). One of the places he most loves to be lifted to is the mantel over the fireplace. This contains several items: the clock with the little airplane circling the dial, several photos, vases (don't touch) and small scented candles. Nicolas especially fancies the photos, of him and his brother mainly. He'll say, "Bébé!" (French pronunciation) admiringly. Then he picks up the candles, one by one, sniffs each with gusto, holds each under my nose and says, "mell!"

I remember vividly when Alexander was this age and first doing and saying things like this. When *cute* happened, the earth seemed to move, and we summoned the media. In other words, we pulled the Camcorder out of the closet, ordered double sets of photographs, and e-mailed the relatives. But now that Nicolas is achieving the same, or greater feats, than his older brother did, there isn't nearly as much fanfare. Some might say this is only what you should expect with a second child: the novelty has worn off.

Indeed, some of my friends clearly thought I was going way overboard as I acclaimed Alexander's accomplishments, particularly friends who were related to a lot of little kids. However, I think my friends were only half right: our mistake was not in celebrating Alexander's attainments—it's in failing to make just as big a to-do about Nicolas's. I believe that God exults when God beholds each bit of growth of each child everywhere. Every child whose senses capture afresh what a remarkable world this is—"mell!"—delights God, the source of all those remarkable candle making materials and rocks and twigs. If we want to follow God, who is in so many ways a grandparent, we would be just as delighted.

FORTY

HANK

"There ain't no rules around here! We're trying to accomplish something!"
(Thomas Edison)

Like most children, Alexander is a selective eater. There are many foods he will not touch, but there is one he cannot get enough of.

Many years ago in Maine Ruth and I had breakfast in a small town diner. The muffins, made from two common boxed cereals, were so good that I asked for the recipe and, surprisingly, they shared it with me. Back home, we tried it once, filed it in the recipe box, where it got shuffled to the back and was soon forgotten. Until I became a grandfather.

Thinking that Alexander, who at the time consumed only banana slices, plain rice, and raw carrots to earn his chocolate pudding, might like them, I made some prior to his arrival. I wasn't even sure he would try them. He not only tried them, he loved them and begged for them three or four times a day. They were virtually all that he ate during the entire visit. I found myself making muffins after he went to bed so he would have fresh ones the next morning. When he returned home, thoughtful Lisa, so as not to weaken the potency of our bond, refused to make them for him. Therefore, when I visited the next time, my very first activity was to make a batch. Maine muffins became a tradition.

When he was four, I invited him to help me make them. I don't know what inspired me to enlist his services. Perhaps God simply tapped me on the shoulder that day. I looked the other way when he dug into the flour with his hands, laughed when the egg he was stirring spilled, and let him taste the sugar with his fingers before we added it. Alexander had a great time. *I* had a great time despite the mess, which was only a minor inconvenience.

After that, making muffins became something we always did together. It became a matter of routine that when muffins dwindled to one or two, Alexander would climb up on his chair and assist me in baking more. Despite all the other activities we engaged in together, this became the one that most defined our relationship.

Recently, I asked if he wanted to make muffins and he, in the middle of a favorite video, shook his head *no*. I already had them in the oven when he came bursting in to announce that he had finished his show and was now ready. When I told him that they were mixed, measured out, and in the oven, he burst into tears and was inconsolable for many minutes. Never have I enjoyed hugging a child more. Never have I enjoyed seeing someone cry so much.

I remember very little of my grandfather. He was the sick man in the mysterious, dark room next to the kitchen, and I had to be quiet all of the time when I was visiting my Grandmother. I try to imagine Alexander years from now making muffins with his grandson and telling him about the many times he made them with his grandpa. The recipe with Alexander's name on it is in the lock box with my will. It is surely the more important document.

FORTY-ONE

RUTH

"Training is everything. The peach was once a bitter almond; cauliflower is nothing but cabbage with a college education." (Mark Twain)

Parents who want to make sure that their child is eating nutritiously and begin monitoring what that child is consuming from the table as soon as solids are possible are destined for a few years of food hell.

"How about chewing two carrots for one vanilla wafer?" I bargain. "Would you eat one half of your tofu sandwich for two pieces of chocolate?" I plead. Food likes and dislikes create situations of endless negotiation between Alexander and me. This is nothing new. I fought the same endless food battles with my own son not too many years ago.

In some households there is no negotiation. Warnings are given, punishment is threatened, or when all else fails, the child is sent to his or her room. These are short-term solutions that don't work. Kids have emotional attachments to certain types of foods. Did you ever hear of a child who hates ice cream but loves broccoli? Television advertisements don't help. They drive the desires of a young appetite.

Gregory, the Terrible Eater speaks to children about the concern that their parents and caregivers have about eating habits. Mitchell Sharmat tells of Gregory, who is not your average goat because he likes to eat such things as fish, eggs, fruit, carrots, and cereal. Gregory's parents want him to eat goat food. They take him to Doctor Ram, who suggests giving Gregory, the picky eater, one new food each day. That night his mother puts a shoelace in his spaghetti. Gregory begins to like new tastes. As Gregory begins to eat more foods that his parents feel are healthy for a young goat, Gregory's parents are greatly relieved.

My grandsons have definite likes and dislikes where food is concerned. They both love fruit and chocolate. Meat and especially vegetables in the case of Alexander are less favored, the one exception being carrots. The texture of food is very important to Nicolas. He likes to eat foods from his tray after giving them the finger test and enjoys a wider range of foods than Alexander. Negotiations are used from time to time, and Alexander will usually go for any deal where chocolate is the barter. Whether that is lucky or unlucky is yet to be determined.

FORTY-TWO

JIM

"It was you who created my inmost self, and put me together in my mother's womb; for all these mysteries I thank you: for the wonder of myself, for the wonder of your works." (Psalm 139: 13-14)

Alexander's father is an airline pilot; part of his professional preparation was to get a degree in aeronautical engineering. On Alexander's mother's side of the family—where I am—people tend to be mathematically challenged but verbally talented. Another trait that shows up all over this family is stubbornness. Come to think of it, stubbornness is not unknown on his father's side either.

I thought I saw this constellation of genes shining out in Alexander very early in his life. We had already traced various facial features and body parts to members on both sides of the family, of course. Alexander has his father's coloring and compact build and his mother's nose. Then one evening I thought I saw the aforementioned psychological characteristic showing up. Mind you, Alexander was perhaps nine months old at the time. He was in his high chair, and I was feeding him. For some reason, which I no longer recall, it was just the two of us there, working together.

What he was eating was something fairly bland and mildly unappetizing, like Mashed Carrots, and Peas and Corn. Not all together; two different heaps. Early on he got me into the rhythm: a spoonful of carrots, and then a spoonful of Peas/Corn. After a while he was satisfied with my performance and became inattentive. His eyes were focused somewhere in the middle distance, for all the world as if he was reading an invisible newspaper or magazine just over my shoulder.

Just to be evil, as is the way of grownups in positions of control, I decided to see what would happen if I got cute with the feeding regimen. So, without fanfare, I tried to give him two spoonfuls of carrots in a row. With the merest gesture, he put me in my place and showed he was the genetic product of firm, orderly people. Without even looking at me, he raised one hand in a policeman's "Halt"; and not resuming eye contact, he waited until I got back on track before he opened his mouth for the next spoonful of Peas and Corn. I reflected that we are who we are, who God made us to be, from the very start. Each of us can be only that one person, and God has made sure that the universe won't have to go without us.

FORTY-THREE

HANK

"There is no fear in love; perfect love drives out all fear."
(1 John 4.18)

I have never seen Alexander really afraid. Oh, he grabs your leg when a strange dog barks or comes near. He talks about the time he had to leave the theater because *A Bug's Life* was too intense for him, and he warns you ahead of time not to read a book to him when he knows that a scary ghost appears in the story. But in day to day living, he exhibits a healthy lack of apprehension and jumps into activities with a fearless gusto.

This is partially due, in my opinion, to the fact that Lisa is a wonderful mother. She gave up a career with a fine income to raise her two sons and has never expressed regret about the enhanced lifestyle that she could have had instead. As the time for formal schooling nears, she worries out loud about which school is best. The local public institution is outrageously overcrowded. Private schools, including those which instruct in French, are distant and expensive. She frets when Alexander doesn't take to a learning game. She has mastered the teaching of Kindermusik in order to be a part of their education. She ran Play Park, an indoor playground for area children, who live in a rainy climate. She plans to be a classroom volunteer when her boys are in school. She spends her days feeding, running to activities, hugging, encouraging, admonishing, and laughing at antics. She's a totally engaged caregiver.

Where did she acquire this dedication and these skills? I found the answer one day while I was playing bridge.

When Nicolas was a newborn and visited St. Louis for the first time, his introduction to the family coincided with another visit. Lisa's Aunt Norma, who had moved to a small, distant town many years ago, was also in St. Louis. She and her husband Clifford had moved to West Plains when he retired. It was far enough away that contact slowed. Age became a factor. Visits to St. Louis became rare.

When Lisa was a newborn, it became economically necessary for Ruth to return to the classroom. Norma agreed to watch Lisa. Until Ruth became pregnant again and had to resign her teaching position, Norma took care of Lisa. Ruth then started a nursery school to bridge the time until elementary school and all-day first grade made a return to teaching possible for her. Norma became her nursery school assistant. Lisa spent an equal amount of time with each of her two major caregivers.

During Norma's visit she was holding Nicolas when he fell asleep. I, frequently the dummy, sat with her in my line of vision. Several efforts were made to take him from her arms and put him into his bed, but she nodded a silent *no* each time. For more than an hour she sat and rocked Nicolas gently until he woke with a start. He looked up at her questioningly. She hugged him to her and smiled. He yawned and returned to sleep.

Grand slam! Lisa has always known love. Why wouldn't she be the good mother of fearless sons?

Forty-Four

Ruth

"Reading is thinking with someone else's head instead of one's own."
(Arthur Schopenhauer)

Once Alexander made a stuffed bear named Corduroy his constant companion, it was easy to get him to choose bear books for story time. One of the most beloved is Bill Martin's *Brown Bear, Brown Bear*. This book uses rhythm and repetition to teach a child in a fun way to learn the names of colors. As the reader turns the pages, he or she finds surprising animals—monkeys or exotic birds—"looking at you," and at the end a smiling teacher, who is pleased that the child has learned, looks out at the reader.

The first time we shared this book, I read it very slowly and carefully. Alexander immediately liked its predictability. After finishing it, I closed the text and asked him, " What do *you* see looking at you?" Alexander looked around his bedroom, picked an object from his toy box, and responded, "I see a yellow chicken looking at me." I continued to ask the same question, and he was busy looking around to find an appropriate response. As time went on, we modeled the story by repeating the same question, "What do you see?" I would ask it dramatically, pausing to let him think of something. "An animal!" he would exclaim, and I would prompt, "Good! I see a….. monkey." Alexander would yell out a color or a descriptive word. The now familiar game changed with each subsequent reading. "I see a pink.....!" After a search, he would cry, "A pink piggy bank!" Alexander found this game endlessly fun. Over and over again he would pick the bear book for story time.

As an adult I find myself referring to rhymes that I learned as a child such as thirty days has September, or spring forward/fall back to help with setting time changes. The easiest way for children to remember each planet's relationship to the sun is to teach them the nonsense sentence, "My very eager mother just served us nine pizzas." Each beginning letter stands for a planet thus reminding us of both their names and their order in the solar system—Mercury, Venus, Earth, Mars, Jupiter, Saturn, Uranus, Neptune, and Pluto. Remembering the Great Lakes becomes easy using the key word HOMES standing for Huron, Ontario, Michigan, Erie, and Superior.

Most children's books have a hook, a repeated theme, concept, or series of words. The fill-in-the-blank game extends and expands the reading experience. Playing verbal games reinforces the meanings of words. What begins as a game becomes a lesson that leads the child into taking ownership of the ideas that were presented in the book. Rhyme, repetition, and word plays are fun; and they help us all remember.

FORTY-FIVE

JIM

"i thank you god for this most wonderful day" (e. e. cummings)

Now that Nicolas is starting to talk a lot, it's curious to note that he is, in one respect, following closely in Alexander's footsteps, or should that be tonguesteps. Like Alexander, and I suppose like most babies, some of Nicolas's first words have been variations on "Mama" and "Papa." But also like Alexander—and unlike other kids? (I don't know that many)—Nicolas is a Pronoun Kid. His waking hours are a constant stream of demonstratives and finger pointing: "This!" (a new food) and "These!" (found toys) and "Those" (piggy bank coins). More accurately he pronounces them as if he were from the streets of Brooklyn as "Dese" and "Dem"). Sometimes he grabs whatever it is when he shouts "Dis!" and shows the object of his sudden interest to the rest of us to be admired.

Whether this is a unique feature or a commonplace development, I think that both boys have been on to something with their pronouns. A lot of Eastern spirituality deals with attaining just such a sense of the uniqueness of each moment, each object, each person, each event. The Zen Master goes through life grasping and announcing "This!"

Nor is this just an Eastern form of enlightenment. Western thinkers try to get at "This!" as well. I seem to recall that there was a noted philosopher in Europe during the Middle Ages whose fundamental idea was "*haec-ceitas*"—"this-ness." He went through life like a baby, trying to look at things freshly, trying to see what made everything what it was, what made "this" "this." A late millennium, verb challenged President seemed to also exhibit some skill in this regard when he argued that his answer depended upon what his definition of *is* is, as if he must ponder this word each time he uses it.

Whether you buy all this or not, I hope that you will at least learn from our grandchildren the trick of perceiving each individual thing and moment with the surprise and wonder that makes you exclaim, "This!"

FORTY-SIX

Hank

"There is no one on earth who does what is right all the time and never makes a mistake." (Ecclesiastes 7.20)

"Where's Nicolas?" I asked. But I was alone in the room. He had been playing with a car just seconds…a few moments?…ago. But now he was not there. A news article had distracted me for just a minute, and in that minute he had disappeared from the room. One of three adults on the fifteenth floor of this high rise condo, I was not necessarily the one in charge. But I had not been paying attention.

I called again, without real apprehension, to the rest of the family in the adjacent kitchen, "Is Nicolas in there with you?"

Without beckoning, three adults assembled in the hall. The condo was not that big. If not in the living room, dining room, kitchen, then he had to be in one of the two bedrooms, bathrooms, or in the dark laundry room, where he loved to peer into the glass windowed washing machine.

But no. The door to the hallway and the hazardous world beyond was wide open. The elevator to the street, the pool, and sudden violent death was a few steps down that hall, and we all realized that Nicolas was quite capable of reaching the down button. Stanley rushed into the hallway and vanished.

Lisa and I continued to explore empty rooms. We told ourselves that just because the door was opened did not mean that he had left.

Opening closet doors and peering under beds, I flashed unwillingly on the deaths of children in my lifetime. Terry, deceased at ten due to Reyes Syndrome. David, a victim of meningitis. A neighborhood child run over by a school bus. I remembered the time that my own brother, co-author of this book, disappeared from our back yard at the age of three. For one solid hour of panic we searched the area. I had never seen my Mother more distraught. He was found calmly strolling down a sidewalk three blocks away.

Stanley returned carrying Nicolas. He had made it down the hall but not onto the elevator.

I should have sighed with relief and hugged him, but instead I shuddered. What if I had not realized he was not around until it was too late? What if he had made it outside and been led away by a stranger? The media is full of stories of children who disappear.

Our panicked loss was a mere moment or two. What must it be like to spend days, months, even years not knowing what happened to your son or daughter? How could a parent or grandparent ever get over the loss of a child especially when the loss or death could have been prevented had the person in charge been more attentive? I have no answer to that question, and, God willing, I will never know the answer.

FORTY-SEVEN

RUTH

"Our bodies will return to the dust of the earth, and the breath of life will go back to God, who gave it to us." (Ecclesiastes 12.7)

In life's first stage, early childhood, death is not usually a subject for serious consideration. Since Alexander and Nicolas have short personal histories to draw from and little experience with life's downside, each day is fresh and full of surprises. Living for the moment, they frequently change activities because something new is always catching their interest. This is the desired life for a preschool child.

This past school year at the age of seven a girl in my class lost her precious cat due to cancer. She had never had to deal with the loss of a loved one before. Many days she would start sobbing for no apparent reason and tell me how sad she was. As a teacher, animal lover, and friend, I searched for a book that might help her live through her anguish and deal with this inevitable life experience.

The Tenth Good Thing About Barney ended my search. Written by Judith Viorst, this book is about a cat named Barney. He dies near the beginning of the story. The narrator, a young boy, is understandably sad. His mother tells him that it is important to think of ten good things about his cat to share at the funeral. Annie, the next door neighbor, comes over. She and the boy discuss whether Barney is somewhere in heaven or somewhere under the ground. Meanwhile, the boy's father is busy planting a packet of seeds. Father says about Barney, "In the ground everything changes. He'll change until he's part of the ground in the garden." The boy finally comes up with ten good things. His list starts with Barney being brave and ends with his pet in the ground helping flowers to grow.

This book uses all of the important words children need to hear in order to deal with death. I have two copies of this book, one at home and the other at school. If any child needs to hear this story, the book is first shared with all of the students in my class, and then it is sent home for the grieving family to discuss. The other book is on a bookshelf at home in case I need a copy at a moment's notice for our grandsons.

A grownup usually leans on a special friend or relative and a deep religious belief to help cope with the loss of a loved one. Children must depend on trusted adults to guide them through their loss of an animal, a grandparent, or any unexpectedly tragic death. Since death is a new experience for children, their normal fears and sadness must be dealt with.

FORTY-EIGHT

JIM

"Our names will flutter / on these hills like little fires ("Our Children, Coming of Age"—Wendell Berry)

Grandparents love to tell stories, old and new, real and made-up, to their grandchildren. A few days ago I overheard my sister-in-law Ruth telling Alexander about Jack and the Beanstalk, that classic eighteenth century English folk tale. She was telling him that there is a whole series of stories about Jack and other giants besides the one with the hen who laid golden eggs. I'm in the middle of a tempestuous family saga, which I'm inventing for Alexander with his play dinosaurs as the characters, each with a special voice. But there's one story I vowed early on to tell Alexander, but haven't yet, because he's not quite old enough.

It's a family story, but Alexander hasn't quite grasped the concept of relationships yet. When I once tried to tell him that his Grandpa Hank and I were brothers, as he and Nicolas are brothers, Alexander got upset and said, "MY grandpa!"—he thought I was trying to horn in on his rights to Hank. Another concept Alexander is just beginning to get is death, and he will need to get that, too, before I can tell him this story.

It's the story of another brother HIS grandpa Hank and I had. His name was Tim. To help Alexander place Tim, I will say that he looked a lot like me, and there are plenty of pictures to back that up. And he sounded like me, too—we even have a videotape. In personality he was as nice as Grandpa Hank, but funnier and braver than Hank and I put together. I will tell Alexander that he and Tim would have had a good time together because Tim was a teacher and loved little kids.

I may wait until Alexander is a teenager to show the videotape. In it Tim, a year before his death, gives an inspiring talk about living with A.I.D.S. It may make Alexander sad to realize what he missed, since Tim died five years before he was born. But I would want him to realize how much love has been shared in his family, a love that helped to create the warm nest into which he was born. Then Alexander will realize why he has turned out to be a loving person, in his turn.

FORTY-NINE

HANK

"Things are going to get a lot worse before they get worse."
(Lily Tomlin)

If you see my daughter, Lisa, the mother of my beloved grandsons, don't tell her about what follows here. You see, she thinks I'm competent and she trusts me.

When Nicolas was one month old, I, having retired from teaching to write, went for a visit and to help out with domestic tasks. Challenged to muster parenting skills that had lain dormant for more than twenty-five years, I was to stay two weeks.

Near the end of the second week, well into the routine of helping with feeding a newborn and tending to a three-year-old, I was apparently exhibiting above average skills.

Lisa, facing long confinement after I left, asked if I could handle both grandsons for an hour, two at the most, so that she and Stanley could go to lunch with friends.

No problem!

As soon as they left, Nicolas, who had become used to my multiple ministrations, began to whimper. What I didn't know at the time was that he was beginning to get his first cold. I held him and watched with concern as the whimpers became sobs. My attention was not on Alexander, whom I thought to be contentedly drawing pictures with magic markers. I mistakenly decided that Nicolas, who was having difficulty breathing and was wheezing in primal fear, desired to be fed. Holding the caterwauling baby with one arm while juggling the bottle, which needed to be heated and tested, I noticed that Alexander was nowhere to be seen. I peered under the table in the dining area to discover that he had taken a purple marker and made zigzag lines over much of the rug's surface. When I grabbed for the marker, he thought I was intent on a game. Did he run into the next room? Of course not. He ran outside. Then the phone rang.

When the parents returned one hour later, both boys were asleep; and I pretended that nothing of consequence had occurred while they were away.

I believe I even managed a slothful yawn. I didn't tell them about cleaning the rug on my hands and knees while chanting my thanks to a benevolent God that the ink was not permanent. I didn't tell them about Alexander being out of my view while I tried to decide whether to abandon their screaming newborn or take him outside into the February rain on a chase.

Edward Dreschnack wisely observed, "Just about the time a woman thinks her job is done, she becomes a grandmother." I suppose this is no less true for grandfathers, who get to revisit ports-of-call without having to sign on for the full cruise, the second time around.

FIFTY

RUTH

"Don't threaten a child; either punish or forgive him."
(Talmud)

Sometimes Alexander pushes the limits of acceptable behavior by talking back, nit picking, or demanding his way. He loses things like his coat, left at school one day. He teases his brother, protests vehemently or runs and hides when he needs sleep. Recently he took a scissors to Nicolas's hair and left bald patches and tufts that even a professional stylist couldn't fix. Often Alexander is not a good listener. He argues over which foods he wants or will not eat so that mealtime can include tension-producing negotiation. Being typical, his parents daily witness what they judge to be bad behavior. Whether it is Dad's no-nonsense, raised voice speaking in French or Mom's direct voice in English, Alexander is in trouble. Most of the time his parents ask him to sit in the corner with his face to the wall or go to his room to think things over. Alexander protests and will usually want to know in a few minutes if he can come back. When it involves roughing up his brother, Alexander will have to explain what happened and how he might handle it better the next time. Alexander, when serious pressure is applied, will apologize to Nicolas.

Nicolas has his bad days too. Sometimes he is teething, regressing, or has a cold. He doesn't like to ride long distances in a car and, howling, kicks his legs and pushes at the restraints. He helps himself to food, usually with chocolate as the main ingredient, when no one is around to stop him. Some days he feels pushed to the limit by too many visiting grandparents. I always know when he is nearing his limit because he becomes cranky and whimpers. If he doesn't get enough rest, he can make life tough for his caregivers.

Judith Viorst wrote a realistic book, which both children and those in charge of disciplining them can really relate to. The main character's name is especially appropriate here, the title being *Alexander and the Terrible, Horrible, No Good, Very Bad Day*. Judith's Alexander tells all the reasons why he has had a rotten day. "I think I'll move to Australia," he says when he finds only cereal in the box. He goes to school and things don't improve. After school the dentist finds a cavity. The dentist will fix it next week, but Alexander still plans to run away to Australia. Alexander can't find shoes at the shoe store. His Dad won't let him play with his desk items at the office. Considering these negative events, Alexander observes, "My mom says some days are like that. Even in Australia."

When either of my grandsons is having a terrible, horrible, no good, very bad day and I am in charge, I usually try to improve the mood by changing the activity. We try a familiar game, take a walk or head for the swing, sing a song, or lay down. But these are, at best, temporary remedies. Often even a change of activity won't fix the mood, which then must be endured. Grandparents can then legitimately lay claim to a terrible, horrible, etc. too.

FIFTY-ONE

JIM

"Pull me out of this swamp; let me sink no further!" (Psalm 69:14)

One of the first words that Alexander learned to use was "stuck." This puzzled us, because it's not an easy word to say—three consonants, after all. But after he started using it, it was amazing how many situations it applied to. Any time a key didn't fit in a lock—he was also fascinated with keys during this phase—he would say, "Stuck!" When a piece of furniture was too big to move, "Stuck!" When the door to a place he wanted to explore wouldn't open, "Stuck!" When the airplane piece didn't immediately slide into its spot in the jigsaw puzzle, "Stuck!" Sometimes it seemed like an all-purpose baby's cussword.

Under his influence, I began to apply "Stuck!" to various situations in my own life, to occasions in which I might previously have expressed myself more vividly, perhaps with a word one letter shorter than Alexander's favorite. The more I used it, the more I concluded that stuckness is a universal human experience, to the point that "Stuck!" has perhaps become more of a prayer than a cussword (some words and names are used in both praying and cussing, after all).

When Alexander declared something "stuck," I often countered by saying, "No, Alexander, it's not stuck—you're using the wrong key." My response also suggests a universal truth, especially applicable in the world of addiction recovery, everyday problems, misunderstandings, or indeed any spiritual realm. Often what we think is "stuck" just seems that way because we've been using the wrong key, or pushing on the wrong door. Or maybe we're pushing when we should pull, like the kid in the *Far Side* cartoon pounding on the door of the Midvale School for the Gifted, a door clearly marked "Pull."

FIFTY-TWO

HANK

"My mother had a great deal of trouble with me, but I think she enjoyed it."
(Mark Twain)

I had an assigned seat on the plane. Lisa, with the boys, was flying stand-by. As the wife of a pilot, she has the blessing of access to cheap airfares and the curse of being bumped if the plane is full. This time there were only two potentially unfilled seats, so it looked iffy.

I boarded at the last minute, so flustered that I forgot to kiss Ruth, who would not join us until Wednesday, goodbye. When I realized this, half the way down the ramp, I backtracked and caused anxiety to the TWA employee who had only seconds before taken my boarding pass and told me to have a good flight. Security conscious, she watched me warily as I bid a proper farewell and headed back down the ramp. Seated at the window, enjoying a moment of calm, I listened to the flight attendant relay take-off instructions and I abandoned hope.

But then I saw Lisa emerge from behind the first class curtain with Nicolas in one arm. Alexander was trotting behind her. I gave a grateful thumb up as she passed.

Perhaps two minutes later, the flight attendant came forward to tell me that a passenger had graciously offered to switch seats so that I might sit with my grandson. I apologized

119

to the two men I had climbed over just a few minutes before and did it again. Lisa was now seated one row behind me in the middle seat on the other side of the aircraft. Nicolas was on her lap.

Perhaps two minutes later, the same flight attendant came forward to tell me that two passengers, the ones on either side of Lisa, had graciously offered to switch seats with us so that I might sit with my daughter. I moved again.

For two and one half-hours Nicolas listened to the same mundane book five times while I stifled yawns and tried to sound interested. He bounced from lap to lap, ate his weight in pretzels, played peek-a-boo with the person seated behind me, attempted to kick the seat in front of me, played for a few seconds with Playdough and then Matchbox cars, scribbled on a pad with markers, resisted every attempt to get him to sleep, and struggled to be let down in the aisle. In other words, he acted like a typical toddler.

I looked over at the lady in the aisle seat who had switched with me. She was engrossed in a book and enjoying a cocktail. I experienced serious envy, but then I meditated deeply about responsibility and the need to endure while Nicolas bounced on his mother's lap. Balance restored, I thanked God that we were not on our way to Australia and took him back.

As the plane touched down, Nicolas, of course, fell asleep. Carrying him up the ramp, I recalled the many times Lisa brought Alexander to visit us under similar circumstances, and then *both* grandsons. I felt a rush of insight, then awe, and finally love. Now I knew.

FIFTY-THREE

RUTH

"Sleep, riches, and health to be truly enjoyed, must be interrupted." (Jean Paul Friedrich Richter)

Sleep. Glorious, refreshing rest. Alas, not to be had when young grandchildren are in town. They beckon Hank and I by six-thirty a.m. each and every morning despite the fact that we have stayed up the previous night to have a little adult conversation with our own children. I see the wisdom in my brother-in-law Don's number one rule of survival, "When they go to sleep (his two grandsons), I do too. Whenever that is." Sometimes Alexander will hop up on our bed ready to play or just talk. Nicolas will call from his crib. In fact, it was in just this circumstance that we heard the word Paca, his name for Hank, clearly for the first time. Nicolas likes to be cuddled when he gets up and before he starts his busy day of exploring. Then he heads for the refrigerator, grunts, and points at the closed door. He wants juice.

At the other end of the day, Alexander is as sleep deprived as the adults, but he is four years old and sleep is his enemy rather than a friend. Since he refuses to take a nap, he nods off at the dinner table in an upright position with food in his mouth. Then he denies that he is sleepy a short time later when he is ready for bed.

When we visit in winter and it gets dark by late afternoon, Alexander wants me to lie in his bed with him and look up at the ceiling. It is blue with lots of softly radiant stars, which glow when other lights are turned off. A round dome halogen light, glowing like the moon, completes the illusion of being outdoors at night. There is something about this ceiling that encourages Alexander to tell what is on his mind. He asks endless questions that he has stored up. We spend a lot of time looking up at the ceiling and talking instead of sleeping when we visit.

A sleepover becomes a big event to Ira and Reggie in the charming tale *Ira Sleeps Over* by Bernard Waber. A major discussion develops over whether Ira should take a teddy bear over to his friend Reggie's house. Mother and father think taking Tah Tah is a great idea. Sister smugly says, "Reggie will laugh. He will think Ira's a baby." Sister prevails. Reggie makes big plans for the evening's entertainment. The anticipation of a fun sleepover builds. After games, wrestling matches, and pillow fights Reggie's father says it is time for bed. A round of ghost stories causes Reggie to take a fuzzy mystery object out of his drawer. It is his teddy bear Foo Foo. Ira quickly runs home to get his bear. When Ira returns, hoping to hear the end of the ghost story, Reggie is fast asleep.

FIFTY-FOUR

Jim

"He took the child into his arms and blessed God; and he said:
'Now, Master, you can let your servant go in peace.'" (Luke 2: 28-29)

Like the airplanes he loves to play with, make the sounds for, and unfailingly observe in the sky, when it comes to sleeping, it's take-offs and landings that are trouble spots for Alexander. He hates to go down for a nap and, as a result, often falls asleep sitting up at the supper table with a forkful of macaroni and cheese halfway to his mouth. Later, while the adults visit in the den below his bedroom, Alexander makes frequent trips down the steps to announce that he cannot sleep. It's no wonder that he's cranky and slow to wake up the next morning.

One hot summer afternoon, I was minding the store by myself while Alexander was down for a nap. His parents and whichever grandparents were in town that day were out, and I was enjoying the newspaper as much as the rest. I heard him fussing, and went upstairs to his room. He both wanted out of his bed and to burrow under his blanket. In other words, he didn't want to wake up just yet, but he needed some kind of change. What I finally hit upon was taking him downstairs and stretching out on the sofa with Alexander lying on my chest.

He has always been too active to be very cuddly, and at the time he was almost too big for this to work. But on this one rare occasion, conditions were just right, and he fell back to sleep in my arms, heart to heart. I eventually dozed off a little myself, and we both had a brief nap out of it. But before I drifted to sleep, I realized, as humans do too infrequently, that I was completely at peace and completely happy, and that I would never forget this moment. It transcended time. If you buy my idea that God is a grandparent, then what God remembers about His relationship to us is revealed in moments like these.

FIFTY-FIVE

HANK

"We grow neither better nor worse as we get old, but more like ourselves."
(May Lamberton Becker)

When I see Alexander and Nicolas side by side on the sofa eating popcorn and engrossed in a Bugs Bunny cartoon, I can see a family resemblance; and it is easy to think they are much alike. But this is simply not the case. They have been themselves, as in very different, from the day of birth. When I compare Nicolas to his big brother at the same age, twenty-two months, the differences are far more notable than the similarities.

Alexander's nature is mercurial, passionate. Prone to meltdowns, he had three that I witnessed during a one-year period and many more that I only heard about. They are now a thing of the past, but his emotions are expansive and always just below the surface. His laugh is hearty, robust and at full volume.

Nicolas is sweet and even-tempered, easy going, and social. He has a lilting, merry chuckle. I have never seen him extremely angry or really distraught, only fretful.

Alexander loves media. As he approached his second birthday, he watched Barney, Corduroy, and Wallace and Gromit as often each day as his parents would permit. His play is rich in fantasy, as my brother, master of all things dinosaur, will attest to.

Nicolas is not especially interested in television or children's videos. He spends his time exploring. He loves to open drawers, manipulate objects, and study the consequences of his actions. I'm surprised that his first two words weren't, "What if...."

Alexander will sneak up and pummel the daylights out of you. Nicolas will come running over and kiss you.

Alexander will reject a new food because of the way it looks. He would be content to eat the same thing three times a day. Nicolas will put something new in his mouth, savor it for a long time, and usually request more. He loves to try a new food. At the same age Alexander was addicted to vanilla shakes. Nicolas is too experimental to focus on just one taste.

Alexander heads for the swings first at any playground, and he loved the to and fro of his rocking horse. Nicolas will spend his playground time looking for wheels to spin, poles to touch, and stairs to climb. He doesn't like to be confined in a swing that just goes back and forth.

In the morning Nicolas will talk to himself for a long time and wait for you to come in to lift him out of his bed. Upon awakening at the same age, Alexander would call out and demand that you come get him, and the hope that you might be lucky enough to doze off again evaporated.

Alexander would most likely go and find another toy to play with if an aggressive child grabbed his and ran. Nicolas would hold on to it tenaciously and howl until the grabber gave up.

Are there similarities? Of course. Both boys have their own personal bears and love chocolate. They also love the water, family projects, outings, and chasing croquet balls in the basement. But these are activities that would probably entertain any siblings of the same sex.

I'm reasonably sure that some of their differences are due to birth order, parental adaptation to increased family size and its resulting demands, and relationship changes. But most seem inherent.

It is fun to watch them grow up with enough time to really observe the uniqueness of each of my grandsons, and I hope to have the opportunity to see them become men. I want to be there to see them approach the podium to receive their Academy Awards for the movie of the year. Alexander will have written the script and Nicolas will have produced.

Fifty-Six

Ruth

"Every baby born into the world is a finer one than the last." (Charles Dickens)

The first time Alexander experienced birth was at Craig School, where I teach. It was springtime. Alexander came to visit my classroom. A kindergarten teacher and friend of mine had eggs in an incubator. Alexander sat like an expectant father with his nose pressed close to the glass. Each time an egg moved or a chick hatched, he took pride in recounting the babies and expressed concern for each one's well being. As the chicks dried their feathers and became more active, my co-worker graciously agreed to send two chickens home in a box over the weekend so that Alexander could monitor their progress and learn to care for them. He lovingly but endlessly changed their water and made sure the level of food in the dish did not stray from the very top edge of the container. Alexander talked to the baby chicks all day, and their well-being was the first thing he attended to in the morning. They were the recipients of his final goodnights at bedtime. Towards the end of the weekend, he wanted to know exactly where the chicks would go when they left his care and who would protect and nurture them.

We shared an appropriate book that very same weekend, *Chickens Aren't The Only Ones*. Ruth Heller's story tells about the many creatures that start life inside an egg. Every bird, most snakes, lizards, turtles, and crocodiles produce babies by hatching them. Dinosaurs did too. Frogs, toads, salamanders, fish, spiders, snails, and many insects can be added to the list. Even two mammals, the spiny anteater and the duck-billed platypus, which are native Australians, lay eggs and hatch their young. This large book with beautiful colored pictures that cover most of each page holds the interest of the very young.

When we finished each page, I would ask, "What do you think would be inside a turkey egg? Alexander would catch the clue and answer correctly, so he became confident that he could give right answers. After he returned to his home in Vancouver, the weekend chick visitors gave us a topic for lots of phone conversation for several weeks. I continued to supply information about their growth and development because Alexander had a genuine interest in the subject. He learned, for example, that white chicken feathers replace yellow down as the bird matures.

Since they are not recommended as long term pets, twenty-one chicks and Alexander's special two went to live on farms. Time moved on to the next group of urban children, who today have little or no exposure to farm animals. I am glad that my school can make the incubation process a first hand experience for them.

FIFTY-SEVEN

JIM

Wisdom says, "I was ever at play in God's presence, at play everywhere in God's world, delighting to be with the human race." (Proverbs 8:30-31)

Sometimes God is peering over my shoulder when I'm looking for presents for the boys. Last Christmas, for instance, I slipped away from a retreat I was giving and drove to a big toy store in a nearby mall. Nothing spoke to me, but I remembered that sometimes when Alexander and I played night-night, he would growl and say a dinosaur was coming to attack us. Not knowing that he had recently gone into a phase of intense dinosaur fascination spurred in large part by the stegosaurus in Ruth's classroom, I got him a box full of highly detailed, plastic dinosaurs.

As time has gone on, those dinosaurs have turned into a game—or, more precisely, into a whole family saga. One of the dinosaurs was blue-green and somewhat prim, so one day I gave it a mother hen, Julia Child voice and a full complement of soap-opera-worthy problems. Alexander and I were off to the races. He named the tyrannosaur "Sharp-tooth" after a cartoon he'd seen. At first Sharp-tooth was thoroughly unpleasant, causing all kinds of mayhem that required the services of Alexander's emergency vehicles—fire-trucks, ambulances, and the occasional beach buggy, in a pinch. But as the story has gone on, and on, Sharp-tooth has evolved into a paterfamilias, a little grumpy but basically good. When he dines, rarely now, on another of his species, he begs, "Give me a break; I'm a dinosaur!" Now, to justify all those emergency services, Sharp-tooth is subject to more medical woes than Job, which gives the "Lady Dinosaur" plenty of chances to emote. A goofy yellow dinosaur has been pressed into service as the family physician; to help him, I've given the triceratops, who looks mildly discontented to me, a nasal, Elaine May voice and the job of the doctor's receptionist.

Now, whenever Alexander sees me, he brandishes a dinosaur and says, "Make it talk!" Happy to oblige.

Sigmund Freud once said that a person possessed, or had regained, psychic health if the person could love and work. Someone else, perhaps thinking this was too Germanic, amended it to "love, work, and play." I have never been very good at playing. So one of the many gifts that Alexander has given me is the chance to learn how to play. I can't do Legos, like Hank, or tell stories interactively, like Ruth. But with my peculiar imagination I can make dinosaurs talk.

FIFTY-EIGHT

Hank

"The three stages of a man's life: He believes in Santa Claus; He doesn't believe in Santa Claus; He is Santa Claus."
(unknown)

We had just gone to have the first professional family portrait taken of four proud grandparents, one loving uncle, two sleep deprived new parents, and one baby. Alexander was three months old, and we had gathered for his first Christmas. The photographer was so good at making nonsense noises that Alexander smiled on each exposure. I have the proof.

After this we went to REI, a sporting goods store, because the other men were going skiing. Not a skier, I wandered up and down the aisles looking at merchandise I had little interest in.

Then I saw them. The boots. A pair of tiny, tiny Nikes on a sale table. They were absolutely impractical. They would fit, perhaps, a two-year old, whose feet had to be just the right size and shape. They were incredibly cute, but the odds that Alexander's feet would become just the exact size needed for them to fit properly were statistically off the chart. I talked myself out of them and wandered some more, but a fixation had taken hold. They were so cheap, I told myself, that, even if they never did fit, it was not a severe loss. And just maybe he'd grow into them and they would be perfect. I tried to imagine how he would look at two, playing in the snow, in

SECOND HELPINGS

these boots. My FIRST solo present. MY first present. I circled the boots again. They had grown cuter and actually seemed a bit more practical. The price was so reasonable too! A woman passed by and I shielded the shoes from her lest she make a grab for them. Completely hooked, I bought them and waited to show them off until evening, when Lisa couldn't quickly and easily make a return. I lost track of these boots and don't know if Alexander ever wore them. I don't want to know.

Two years later, we were shopping in a store in Annapolis, Maryland. Ruth came over and said, "I want to show you something." What the something turned out to be was a night light in the form of a charming, coastal lighthouse. We were both enamored. Reason didn't matter. Difficulty of transport due to its fragility didn't matter. We had to have it regardless of cost or impracticality.

It sits on Alexander's chest of drawers and is turned on every night. I like to think that he wakes from a bad dream, sees it, is calmed, and returns to sleep. I want to believe that he has not stumbled or fallen in the dark because our lighthouse illuminates his way. I don't know if either of these scenes has ever happened. I don't need to know.

What I want to and need to know is why grandparents buy expensive and impractical gifts for grandchildren that they, as parents of young children, would never have even considered for one second.

FIFTY-NINE

RUTH

"God gave us memories so that we might have roses in December." (James M. Barrie)

Little boys are natural collectors, and weather is a scientific wonder, which affects us all. This seems like a sentence with two thoughts that do not go together, but they do. For proof, seek the truisms explored in *Snowballs*.

For our grandsons, who like to spend most of their day outside, weather dictates the kind of play that they choose. In the summer they have fun in the portable backyard pool. In the fall they jump in the leaves. In the winter they enjoy the snow or sledding down a steep hill up at Timberline Lodge. In the spring they dig in the dirt and plant. And each activity has its equipment.

Once when Alexander was visiting in May we had an unusual hailstorm, one to be remembered. Alexander was in the tub when all of a sudden a terrific noise was heard on the roof. Grandpa quickly wrapped Alexander, and they ran outside to see what the commotion was about. There were ice crystals the size of grapes hiding in the bushes, collecting around the fence, pinging off the sidewalk, and covering the lawn. Alexander, who had never seen hail, wanted to touch it. Once was not enough. He kept reaching to the ground for more. It was very dark, cold, and slippery, but Alexander kept insisting that he wanted to stay outside.

There are many wonderful children's books about weather. Lois Ehlert, for example, has written two beautiful ones on the subject. *Red Leaf, Yellow Leaf* is a visually gorgeous book about fall, but our grandsons favor her later book called *Snowballs*. In it a child saves all the treasures that he finds on a daily basis in a bag. He eventually uses them to decorate snowmen. To demonstrate that snowmen (or should I say snow*persons* to be current) seem very big to the young child, the author cleverly makes the reader turn the book vertically to read the pictures and words. When the sun comes out and the snowpeople begin to disappear, Lois Ehlert tells about snow and the three forms water can take.

After reading this book, I turned the experience into a little science experiment. We heated water for hot chocolate on the stove, and I talked about liquids, solids, and gasses. I pointed out how heated water turns to a gas and disappears into the air as steam. Alexander knew that if we put the same water into the freezer, it would become ice cubes. This kind of activity can lead to an explanation of how snow is created, or in our case hail. The final pages of photographs and text in *Snowballs* helped.

Avid junk collectors in every season, both of my grandsons like to point to all the things they see on the snowmen in the book, and this encourages them to share their junk collection with me. "How could you use that plastic fork to decorate your snowman?" I asked, starting an interesting dialogue.

SIXTY

JIM

"Let all the earth praise God: sea monsters and all the deeps, fire and hail, snow and mist, storms that obey God's decrees." (Psalm 148:7-8)

Alexander's fourth year with me has been much about dinosaurs, and especially about the box of predators and gentle herbivores I gave him a year ago. As Those Dysfunctional Dinosaurs are coming up on their second Christmas with the family, there have been some striking developments in the saga that Alexander and I are creating around them. No reindeer games for us.

First, I am happy to announce that we had a double wedding at Thanksgiving. We have achieved relative calm instead of the endless mayhem that characterized the early part of the saga, including many ambulance trips to the Dinosaur General Hospital and many life-and-death surgeries. Sometimes before the operation T. Rex was alive, sometimes dead, not an irreversible condition in the saga. Anyway, the T. Rex Father finally married the Lady Dinosaur. Why they hadn't married before, with all their children as the world turns in the days of our lives, was a matter we didn't pursue. At the same time the Doctor Dinosaur and the Nurse Dinosaur also married. Steggie, the Stegosaurus, who surprised us on this occasion by turning out to be a dinosaur of the cloth, performed the ceremony.

Second, my Thanksgiving with Alexander and Nicolas ended on an appropriately festive note. We went on our second annual Christmas tree hunt and found a beauty in the woods. While his parents were putting on the lights, a necessary first step, Alexander got impatient for the next phase of decoration, the ornaments. So I suggested that we set up the manger scene. Alexander's family's main stable is split-level, and for some reason Alexander insisted on crowding most of the dramatis personae, shepherds and wise men both, on the cramped upper level. After we succeeded in shoehorning in the last shepherd, his parents were still stringing lights. So, inevitably under the circumstances, we set up the dinosaurs in a reverent half-circle outside the stable. I put the pterodactyl at the peak of the roof, in the place usually reserved for the proclaiming angel.

I hope that when Alexander is older and hears in church about all creation worshipping God that he will think of our manger scene and be glad for the richness of His planet through all of its long ages.

SIXTY-ONE

Hank

"Don't ever take a fence down until you know why it was put up." (Robert Frost)

In the order of things, Ruth is the designated reader. I cannot begin to match her knowledge of or enthusiasm for children's literature, so I defer to her at reading time.

But there are times when she is not around, and I get to share Alexander's reading hour with Stanley, who always has an impressive number of age-appropriate French books piled on the bedside table.

Bathed and brushed, Ali was waiting expectantly in bed with the pillows pummeled and propped just right when I came in empty-handed. I asked him to select a book; and he disappeared, returned, and scrambled quickly back into position with one I had never seen before. We snuggled in and I began. By page two I was stifling a yawn because the book was awful. Turgid yet dull. I could barely keep my mind on a story with no discernible plot or interesting characters. Their names and the vocabulary, I thought to myself, were more suited to a book for adults. I suspected the writer was showing off.

It was long too. Half way through I asked Alexander if he wanted me to finish the story. Despite what I assumed was obvious, my dislike for it, he nodded avidly in the affirmative; and I realized that despite my poor performance he was riveted to the dumb thing. I slogged through on automatic and managed to stay awake until it was time for a French tale. Stanley and I changed places.

I went into the living room where Lisa was drinking tea and enjoying at nine p.m. her first few moments of the day that didn't involve parenting. "I just read a dreadful book," I began; and before I could finish my review, Lisa named it. I was surprised speechless. She had no way of knowing what I had read.

Lisa continued, "At the bookstore I told Alexander that he could pick out any book, and that's the one he selected. He asks me to read it to him often."

"Does he know how sappy and predictable it is?"

"No, he loves it," she said simply, ending the discussion.

I mulled this over and wished that I had tried harder to like it, or at the very least to have asked Alexander before I began to read why he had chosen it. That way I might have understood its appeal to him and done a better job of reading it. I decided that I must be genuinely clueless about what children like. But then I recalled all the books we had shared, and loved, together. I also recalled the many times when one friend or another had pressed me to read a book, which I found not to my taste and either had to slog through or skip read so that it would seem like I had read it, just to please them. Reading preferences are, above all, a matter of background and interests. Returning borrowed books is the hardest part since I must convey in equal measure both guarded enthusiasm and basic honesty. It becomes an exercise in sparing someone's feelings. The same courtesy should extend to children.

SIXTY-TWO

Ruth

"Smiling faces make you happy, and good news makes you feel better." (Proverbs 15.30)

Alexander walked across the street and then ran toward me. "Come on, Grandma," he shouted. "The cat just had kittens." What excitement filled the air!

We re-crossed the street and knocked on the door. Sure enough, many feeding kittens were snuggled close to their mother. The neighbors had moved the birthing box into the living room so that the children up and down the block could get a look at the newborns. Alexander circled this box and then went down on his knees to get a closer look. The mother cat did not seem to mind if he just watched. She did not even mind when her owner placed a kitten in Alexander's eager hands. Since others soon heard the news, a crowd began to form; so we did not stay too long. We chattered on about the kittens as we walked home.

This was the perfect time to hear a tale called *Koko's Kitten*, the book that made Alexander laugh harder than any other book I have read to him, by Dr. Francine Patterson. What an amazing, true story! The author taught a female gorilla named Koko how to communicate with humans using the hand and body gestures of American Sign Language. When Koko was twelve, Dr. Patterson asked her what birthday gift she wanted. Koko signed, "Cat." Using a blow test, Koko selected a tailless tabby from a group of three and named her kitten All Ball. Koko took loving care of her new charge. Even when the aggressive kitten would scratch or bite, Koko would not harm All Ball. A good gorilla mother, she combed, petted, and kept the kitten clean. Koko liked to play tickle, chase or blow-it games and provided lots of warmth, affection, and attention as All Ball grew. One December morning a car hit the kitten. He died instantly. Koko grieved as a human parent would. While being moved and entertained, the reader learns a lot about the work of the Gorilla Foundation. There are photos rather than drawings to accompany the story.

Alexander went to see the kittens across the street often. As they grew and matured very quickly, the neighbor had no trouble finding owners for all of the babies. Alexander stills visits the mother cat. Contact with pets is important for the young. Stroking a dog gently or listening to a cat purr contentedly because of the way it is being treated builds compassion for living creatures. Keeping an animal from harm and filling a pet's bowl with water and food are ways to teach responsibility. When Alexander has his choice of a house pet, I think he will choose a dog; but for now he surely doesn't miss an opportunity to play with the feline across the street.

SIXTY-THREE

JIM

"Too long have I lived among people who hate peace, who, when I propose peace, are all for war." (Psalm 120: 7)

As Ruth has made clear in her essays, Alexander has had a great deal of fine children's literature read to him. In fact, he has often heard the same stories in English and in French. Both Ruth and Marjorie love to read Robert Munsch's lovingly rendered *Love You Forever*, which is available in a French translation, to him. That and careful screening of his home TV consumption has preserved, to the degree that it is possible, his innocence. He has been protected from a lot of the mechanized violence that shows up in countless movies and TV shows, many ostensibly designed for children. In toy departments he loves to handle and study the action figures, usually with pumped up muscles and posed to fight, that are tied in to those shows. They're mostly all sharp, pointed weaponry and geometric parodies of the human face, often sneering. Sometimes he begs to have these figures, but his parents remain firm. Elsewhere you'll read the story of Alexander saying he couldn't take the first (G-rated) movie he saw in a theater because "I'm just a little boy."

So I was a little surprised at Thanksgiving when it came time for me to do some bedtime reading that the book Alexander chose was *Godzilla vs.*—well, Godzilla was versus several unpleasant creatures, the only one of which I recall was the Smog Monster. I wondered how this ringer had gotten in with his Babar and Curious George collections. Later I learned that Godzilla happened because at some point he was given a choice of any book he wanted to buy. He must have learned about Godzilla from other kids he has met, or maybe all our Dinosaur Games have made him a sucker for a book with what looks like a particularly lurid dinosaur on the cover. Anyway, I read it to him every night during this visit and learned later that he requests it at least once a week from his regular readers.

When he first handed it to me to read, I made the best of it. I tried to camp up the reading, first by barking out the story as if badly dubbed from Japanese, and then by giving funny voices to some of the characters. Alexander found the bad dubbing mildly amusing, but quickly put a stop to the comic voices: "You sound like the Nurse in our Dinosaur Game!" And he told me to stop shaking the book, which I had done to mimic the geological events that Godzilla was causing.

In the end, the sad fact is this. It's probably better that he learn that the world is often a violent place than remain in the gentle Eden of Barney and Arthur. I just wish it didn't have to be at bedtime.

SIXTY-FOUR

Hank

"Every person needs recognition. It is expressed cogently by the child who says, 'Mother, let's play darts. I'll throw the darts and you say, 'wonderful.'"
(M. Dale Baughman)

Mary, our next door neighbor, gave us a Step 2 gardening truck that she no longer wanted. We have never used it for weeding. Part of our backyard is a hill so steep that we have a lawn service mow it. Due to the terrain, the truck has found its unintended purpose.

Alexander discovered that he could take the little truck, actually a low, portable seat at flower level, up to the brow of the hill and coast down. It was a safe, fun activity because he could grasp the handle on one side, prop his back against the other, and hold his feet out to improve steering and balance on his ride. Were he to spill, he was close enough to the ground to avoid injury. He entertained himself with this activity for great lengths of time. Going slightly higher and coasting from a different angle became the game while Ruth and I sat on the patio applauding and offering encouragement.

One evening at dusk I heard a commotion, looked out, and discovered Alexander's father and my nearly thirty-year-old son Matthew engaged in a contest. Stanley and Matt were taking turns on the Step 2. The tone was still playful, but the impromptu game was heating up alarmingly. The object of the sport was to begin higher on the hill, descend faster, and then coast farther toward the patio. I envisioned a direct hit on a support beam causing the roof to collapse, a concussion or broken limb, or both. But they were having too much fun, so I withheld judgment and became a cheerleader instead of a curmudgeon. All too soon it became deadly serious as machismo took precedence over common sense. In the fading light of the day each racer now disappeared into the forest and came roaring down the hill. I had to close my eyes for each finish. A slightly bent wheel ended the endeavor, and I am too diplomatic to say who won.

During the next visit, neighborhood children gathered in our yard and discovered the same sport. But this time there was edenic cooperation as each child took his or her turn. Spills caused laughter rather than anxiety. One mother pretended to hold up a sign and called out, "Ten!" each time her daughter made a successful run. But it never became, "You're the best!"

When does competition become more important than cooperation? Is it when estrogen and testosterone flow through the floodgates of adolescence? Does it begin when soccer moms and dads call out, "Kick it harder, Jimmy!" I cannot imagine a grandparent who would not be pleased to hear that his or her progeny came in first, won the scholarship, or was voted best. Maybe this is what we mean by *loss of innocence*, the first time we have to win the game instead of simply enjoying it.

SIXTY-FIVE

Ruth

"If you think you can, you can. And if you think you can't, you're right." (Mary Kay Ash)

Our conversation led to a nighttime adventure. It began with my comment that when Grandpa and Grandma went to Australia, we looked for the Southern Cross in the vast sky. "What's that?" Alexander asked. I pondered how to explain and said, "It's a constellation in the Southern Hemisphere." This was beyond the ken of this wide-eyed four-year-old as it would be for most pre-schoolers, so I showed him the Australian flag and pointed to the four bright stars that almost form a cross. I traced this cross with my finger. He understood. I told Alexander that in North America, where we live, we can't see the Southern Cross at night. Alexander, of course, asked, "WHY?" I explained that the curve of the Earth made it impossible to see and talked about the Big Dipper, the Little Dipper, and the North Star; but Alexander had a blank look on his face. So that night we went outside for an astronomy lesson.

When I used the flashlight to pinpoint the three main stars of the Little Dipper, it became immediately clear that Alexander did not know what a dipper was. What child of our high tech culture would know this archaic tool? He needed to see a real dipper and have a demonstration of its use to relate to the configuration in the night sky. After we abandoned the search for the dippers, we looked for the North Star. He could not find it. Luckily, I had the perfect resource inside to go with the hot chocolate. And I had a soup ladle too.

A very good beginning book for children to learn some of the basics about stars is *The Big Dipper* by Franklyn M. Branley. In it a smiling daughter notices that some stars are brighter than others. Her father encourages discovery by leading her to the realization that the sky looks different in summer and winter. The book illustrates the use of a dipper and shows the Big Dipper on the same page. Direction words like north, south, east, and west, difficult concepts for small children, are explained along with the use of a compass. The book gets progressively more difficult, so it is one that Alexander will grow into as he learns about the big and little bears, Ursa Major and Minor, and the other constellations.

To complete his first astronomical experience, we took black construction paper, and Alexander licked silver stars and placed them on the page. We drew a line from each star connecting seven points to make both Dippers. We counted the stars. I made a Southern Cross on my paper so that I could explain again what we had seen in Australia. Alexander now had less trouble understanding. We went outside and searched for the North Star and both dippers. This time he found all three of them on his own.

SIXTY-SIX

JIM

"How much longer will you forget me? How much longer will you hide your face from me? How much longer must I endure grief in my soul?" (Psalm 13:1-2)

One nice thing about being a grandparent is that, unless you actually live with your grandchild, you are not necessarily around for some of his or her darker moments. I had been informed that Alexander, usually cheerful and resilient when I was around him, was nonetheless capable of real meltdowns. We used to call them tantrums in the pre-nuclear age. But I didn't actually see one until we went with his parents to the Seattle Garden Show.

His parents left him with me while they went off to get a newfangled hoe that was selling briskly. It was a Friday evening, and around the displays there was a big, noisy crowd. There were very bright lights on the exhibited gardens, but a lot of darkness and shadows in between, like a horticultural Fun House. Anyway, Alexander lost it. He started sobbing heart-brokenly in my arms; under stress he also went bilingual on me, and kept moaning, *"Ou est maman? Ou est papa?"* (French for "Where is, etc."). I didn't know what to do; passers-by glanced at us either sympathetically or mildly irritated.

Eventually, of course, *"maman"* and *"papa"* came back with their hoe, and that solved all of Alexander's problems.

SECOND HELPINGS

They were probably gone no more than fifteen minutes. Really it's not surprising that he got so upset. One and a half years old, he had unknowingly violated what people in recovery call the "H.A.L.T." rule. He had gotten too hungry; isn't it past my regular feeding time? He had gotten too angry; where are Mom and Dad when I need them? He had gotten too lonely: who is this strange man holding me, and who are all these unknown people noisily milling around me? It was 6:30 P.M. and he hadn't had a nap. Sleep-deprived, he was way too tired to cope with the stimulating scene. Oh, and there was one more problem, which may also strike a chord with recovering people, at least as we look back on our drinking days. He also had a "B" in his pants—for some reason Alexander decided early on that this would be his decorous term for that situation which requires a change of diapers. In any case, this incident left me with a new watchword in the form of a phrase—as you travel life's road, don't get too hungry, angry, lonely, or tired—particularly if you have a "B" in your pants.

SIXTY-SEVEN

Hank

"Mistakes. Life would be dull without them." (Oscar Wilde)

Nicolas is going through the period of maturation that includes what is referred to as separation anxiety. When his Mother is out of sight for even a few seconds, he begins to sob "Mommy" piteously, and he is not placated until he is deeply distracted from thinking of her, or she returns.

I had my first taste of this when Lisa ran back into the terminal to see if she could locate the checked-in box, which the airline had temporarily lost.

Nicolas, strapped into his car seat behind me, had not seen me in three months. While she was gone, he began calling out, "Momma," and pointing to where she had vanished. His anxiety level was rising with his voice.

In the driver's seat where he could not see me, I tooted the horn and pretended great surprise by squeaking, throwing my hands up, and bobbing up and down. Alexander began to laugh. I tooted again, feigned even greater surprise, and Nicolas giggled. We played this game until Lisa returned with the missing box. It surely irritated the travelers who passed us on the way to their cars, but it got us through the moment.

A few days later, Ruth and Lisa went to dinner together leaving me alone for the first time this visit with the boys. When Nicolas realized that his Mother had left, he began whimpering like a puppy on its first night in a new home. Assurances of her return didn't help. Toys didn't work. Having my own anxiety attack, I grabbed a CD called *Kids Dance Party* and advanced to the third track, "Get Up and Boogie." Yes, I danced, and Nicolas, who loves music and rhythm, got up and joined me. Mommy could have gone back to Venus for all he cared. I was glad the shades were pulled, and I didn't tell the returning diners of our impromptu performance.

In Vancouver for the Fourth of July, we emptied a box of fireworks into the night sky. A few days later a misplaced Midwestern storm broke with thunder and lightning. My grandsons' fourteen-year old cousin Damien was visiting from France. We watched the flash and boom from inside the garage. I sensed that Damien wanted to stomp in the rain. Kicking off my shoes and grabbing Alexander in my arms, I beat Damien to the huge puddle forming where the driveway meets the street. For ten or so minutes we cavorted and splashed, having a great time while getting soaked to the skin.

It wasn't until later that I recalled the impressive number of people who have been struck by lightning because they didn't take precautions or acted foolishly. Oh, well, it was too late for regrets, and we survived. Given a similar circumstance, however, I would probably not do the same again.

If it weren't for grandsons I also would never honk my horn, boogie, or play with fireworks. Thank God for them.

SIXTY-EIGHT

RUTH

"If you ask me what I came to do in this world, I, an artist, I will answer you, 'I am here to live out loud.'" (Emile Zola)

  When Lisa was young, we enrolled her in piano classes. She studied and played for many years. Most of the music was classical, which pleased her Father greatly. She did the usual yearly recitals and achieved a measure of success. As she entered the busy teenage years, though, there was less time for practice because her work and school schedules were all consuming. An interest, however, had been set for life.

  Nicolas and Alexander are enjoying the rewards of this interest through participation in the Kindermusik program that Lisa and her friend Julie run in a local church facility. This program, which combines music and a child's need for movement, is wonderful for the young. The children have adults in attendance with them in the beginning; but as they mature, they become independent participants. The classes use the human voice, gestures, and listening activities to build skills. Instruments used include the auto harp, guitar, drums, rhythm sticks, sandblocks, shakers, and cymbals. Activities for the older preschoolers add the glockenspiel, dulcimer, recorder, and homemade music makers.

  One of the early songs that both boys enjoyed was "Roll and Catch." Nicolas would roll a small chime ball to Lisa, and she would catch it and roll it back while they sang. At fourteen months Nicolas could tell by the sound of the music what he was supposed to do. He could even hum the melody. Alexander especially loved the song "Two Little Blackbirds." He sang it over and over again and used his pointer fingers as he sang. Making up new rhymes with the same melody, he inserted the names of his friends. Nicolas, imitating his older brother, sat on the piano bench next to Alexander and hummed along. Alexander, as serious as a concert pianist, hit an occasional note on the keyboard. We saw a child pretending to play the piano, but it was obvious that he actually thought he was an accomplished instrumentalist.

The *Educational Leadership* magazine for November, 1998, contains an interesting article called "The Music in Our Minds." The question explored by the writer, whose surname is Hanshumaker, is "What are the benefits of music?" Music, the writer concludes, has the ability to facilitate language acquisition, reading readiness, and general intellectual development. Music enhances creativity and promotes social development, personality adjustment, and self-worth. Indeed, learning about music is a key developmental skill.

SIXTY-NINE

JIM

"The rockets' red glare, the bombs bursting in air."

On the first couple of Independence Days of Alexander's life, he was put to bed before the excitement started. I learned on the second of these, by the way, that his mother was a considerable daredevil once the fireworks came out. She could easily find employment as a munitions expert for the government, when the boys are older. But for Alexander's third 4th of July, he got to stay up later, until the sun went down and the sparklers were lit. He was living on a friendly and multi-cultural cul-de-sac. Several of the neighbors had younger children, so in the near darkness a small crowd was pulling lawn-chairs up to the curb around the perimeter of the concrete circle and bringing out their personal stash, acquired from roadside stands.

Alexander was already a little spooked to be up late and sitting next to the street at night. When the little firecrackers started going off, he visibly shook and sobbed to be taken back inside the house. I picked him up and tried to assure him that we adults were watching carefully and that everything would be fine. He was unconvinced and tearfully held on to me. What finally turned the tide was a little rocket that ejected a paper parachute at the apex of its short flight. Alexander caught a glimpse of the parachute through his tears and over my shoulder, and he Oooooed with pleasure; and, to seal the deal, I ran to get him the parachute. He was enchanted with it, so of course we shot off all the parachute-enhanced rockets that we had. In his excitement, Alexander forgot to be afraid. Eventually he joined the other kids in waving sparklers; you could see the glitter reflected in his eyes.

Naturally we reserved whatever was our biggest cannon for the very end, and one of the adults, far enough away from the spectators to be a danger, set it off over the cul-de-sac. Like the rest of us, Alexander yelled joyfully when all the colors burst in air. In just one evening he had made the long journey from wanting to withdraw in fear to being one of the excited neighborhood kids who would have trouble settling down and going to sleep. There's nothing like a parachute—even a paper one—to give you a sense of independence.

SEVENTY

HANK

"Grandfather: Someone who when you want something you get it."
(unknown)

"Put it on your list." This is Lisa's standard suggestion to Alexander when he is in a toy store and he is begging for something either worthwhile or a waste of money. Since he was born in September, all summer long it's his birthday list that gets added to. Through the fall and early winter it's Christmas that gets anticipated with a list that outgrows a single page. I suppose we need Children's Day in the spring between Mother and Father's Day to balance Alexander's lists.

It is a natural thing for a child in a consumer culture full of toys and games to want many. As our children were growing up, our standard reply to being hit upon for purchases was, "We'll see." One time Matt, approaching world weary and wise teenagehood, shot back, "That's what you always say! And it means *no*, so why don't you just say it?" I was hurt until I realized that he was right. "We'll see," became a shared family joke.

I think that Lisa's method is better. Putting wishes on a list teaches a child writing skills, the discipline of the delayed reward, and the difference between what he or she really will enjoy over time and what is just a temporary trifle to be dropped if the child is allowed to cull the list.

SECOND HELPINGS

We were in F.A.O Schwarz. After greeting the animated bear who told us to have a really, really good time, Alexander disappeared into the back where the action figures were. I noted stack upon stack of ignored Star Wars tie-ins and wondered why Jar Jar Binks and his cronies had not done well and who was taking the heat for this apparent failure to move product.

Alexander reappeared with a box. "Can I have this, Grandpa?"

I looked it over and it seemed innocuous enough. A Pokemon icon, the latest craze. Cute. Not a menacing figure of violence, reasonably sturdy for lengthy play, and not too expensive. I mulled it over. Normally I would have bought it for him in a flash and thought nothing of it. It's a grandparent's prerogative to treat, as in spoil, grandchildren. But this time I thought the better of it and said, "Put it on your Christmas list, Alexander."

I expected him to persist in a campaign to have the toy NOW!, but he didn't protest. Instead he went back to the shelf, dropped to his knees, and looked at some cool knights and dragons. He became immediately engaged in deciding which of these he wanted for Christmas too.

Neither wisdom nor parenting skills can be taught. They are usually gained through trial and error. Hopefully, each generation in any advancing culture builds on the success of, and hopefully learns from the failure of, the previous one. Delighted to see evolution in action, I cheered Lisa.

SEVENTY-ONE

Ruth

"Children are unpredictable. You never know what inconsistency they're going to catch you in next." (Franklin P. Jones)

Losing a tooth is a big event in a child's life. In a grandparent's life too, for that matter. A story that speaks to the experience of finding your very first wobbly tooth is told in a delightful way in the book called *Little Rabbit's Loose Tooth* by Lucy Bate. Little Rabbit worries about what she can and cannot eat at the table because of a soon to be free front tooth. On Friday it comes out in her chocolate ice cream. "I have a window in my mouth. I can stick my tongue through it," says Little Rabbit. She thinks about a lot of things she could do with her prize. She could make a necklace, or hang it on her wall, or put it in her pocket. She begins to imagine what the tooth fairy might do with the tooth if she places it under her pillow. "Could it be that my tooth will be given to a baby rabbit that was just born?" she wonders. "Could it be that the tooth fairy will put my tooth up in the sky, and that is how stars are made? Perhaps a fairy will chant a magic spell and turn the tooth into money!" Undecided, Little Rabbit puts it in an envelope and waits until morning.

Every time I read this tale, I am experiencing some guilt because it reminds me of an awful day. When Alexander was seventeen months old, I decided to play some nursery tunes on the piano. Placing him on my lap, I intended to balance him there and use my hands to play the keys. He became excited by the sounds and lunged forward to touch their source, the keys. As quick as lightning he tumbled between my legs to the floor. On the way down he managed to bite completely through his tongue with a shiny new front tooth. Blood began to pour from his mouth as he sobbed piteously. Since the blood could not be stanched, Stan and Hank took him to St. John's Hospital. Stitches were definitely needed. Because of his age, delicate surgery was required, and it was performed that evening. He stayed overnight at the hospital for observation. There was fear that the tongue would not heal properly and that speech would not develop in a normal way. A scar remains to remind me.

At the time I was sure that Alexander's parents would never trust me again. Fortunately this was not the case. The tongue did heal, and he learned new uses for his two front teeth, like biting when he became angry or during play. I suppose this is instinctual because most small children go through a biting stage, but it is one of the more unpleasant bad habits to correct while a child is growing up. I wish it were as easy to get rid of bad memories.

SEVENTY-TWO

JIM

"Margaret, are you grieving! Over Goldengrove unleaving?..." (Gerard Manley Hopkins, S.J.)

Every now and then, Alexander, nearly five, will suddenly break down and cry unexpectedly. They say that the writers for "I Love Lucy" knew Lucille Ball's schtick so well that they only had to write, for example, "Puddle up," for stage direction, and the great Lucy would let her face collapse into a tearful heap. Alexander does the same, often when you think that not much of anything is going on.

The other day, for instance, he was fooling around with a rubber snake he had gotten, I believe as a souvenir from Zoo School (where he petted an actual snake and found it remarkably dry). For some reason Snaky had lost a fairly hefty chunk of rubbery scales towards his tail—unless, of course, you think of a snake as *all* tail. Anyway, Alexander's Mom had already tried to reattach the tail with a Band-Aid; this had failed, and she had done it again, this time specifying that, if this Band-Aid went the way of the previous one, that that was it—Snaky was history. She then went grocery shopping. Alexander, like any normal human being of any age, started fussing at the splice. Of course even a sturdy Band-Aid was bound to give way to all that poking and prodding. Soon Alexander stood in the middle of the room, holding a part of Snaky in each hand, calmly noting that this was the end.

And then, suddenly, he "puddled up." It had hit him that Snaky was now officially off life-support and, if he was afforded the ignominious trash burial as threatened, that Alexander would never see him again. I had to hug him and comfort him. In any case the story had a happy ending: Alexander's Uncle Don, a veteran of the foreign service, was visiting, and from his store of overseas skills figured out a way to suture Snaky back together before Mom returned.

I'm glad Don was there. And it's not because Alexander took the rehabilitated reptile to his bosom ever after. Rather, like any normal kid he completely lost interest in Snaky now that the toy didn't have a Band-Aid to pick at. It can be presumed to repose among the other toys put out to pasture. But, like the Jesuit poet Gerard Manley Hopkins and his friend Margaret ("Spring and Fall", to a young child. Márgarét, are you grieving over Goldengrove unleaving?), I see more in Alexander's tears than the vicissitudes of a soon-discarded toy. Alexander was crying because the fact of irrevocable loss suddenly hit him where he lives and stopped him in his tracks. It's bittersweet for me, as it was for Hopkins, to end by saying that Alexander's threatened loss was more or less easily forestalled. This time.

SEVENTY-THREE

Hank

"In every real man a child is hidden that wants to play."
(Friedrich Nietzsche)

Ruth and I were flying home that afternoon. We wanted to take smoked salmon for gifts. The store with the most reasonable price was in Troutdale, about forty-five minutes away. I asked Alexander if he wanted to join me. He did and we arrived at the store at nine a.m.

I freed him from the restraints, and he caromed around the inside of the car. I grabbed him quickly and lifted him out. Having been unable to move for almost an hour, he darted toward freedom as soon as he was let down. My heart skipped a beat since he was heading toward parking lot traffic. I seized him and he squirmed even more to be let down. I carried him to the door of the store and, with my free hand, pulled the handle. It didn't budge. The door was locked. The store didn't open until ten. Ten! TEN!!

Since it was too far back to the house, I decided to wait out the hour. We had no books, no toys, no games. We had just had breakfast, so there was no use going to a restaurant, not a good idea with a three-year old even when he *is* hungry. So I decided we should check out the other stores. Perhaps I'd get lucky and find an opened toy emporium somewhere in this outdoor outlet mall. Alexander had just outgrown his stroller, so we began to walk. Or more accurately, I began to walk. A child, of course, doesn't walk. He runs towards whatever attracts his attention. Like traffic again.

None of the stores were opening before ten, but we did find a patch of grass to wrestle in. Then we circled back and climbed into the car. Although there was no need to strap him in, I must admit I did consider that option as Alexander bounded into the back and bounced on the seat. We played peek-a-boo with the rear view mirror. He climbed into my lap, grasped the wheel, and pretended to drive. I made engine noises. We played with all the knobs on the dashboard.

It became hot in the car so we clambered out and found the drinking fountain we had discovered earlier. It was Alexander's second drink and my first. We had a contest to see who could use his lips to expel the longest stream of water. Then we saw who could shoot water the farthest. Alexander won.

Back in the car we had a rude noise contest. When Alexander erupted in peels of helpless laughter, I figured I had won that one.

Back on the walkway, we looked into each window and talked about the merchandise on display. I made no attempt to wipe off our fingerprints.

Back in the car for only two minutes, Alexander needed another drink. This time he invented a game where he leaned over the sidewalk and saw how long he could hold water in his mouth before letting it flow out in a steady stream onto the concrete. I applauded each effort.

I looked at my watch. Fifteen minutes had elapsed.

It was only in retrospect that this became a great good time.

SEVENTY-FOUR

RUTH

"Laughter is a tranquilizer with no side effects." (Arnold Glasgow)

Baby activities are truly universal. Nicolas gets endless pleasure from playing peek-a-boo or *where is it?* games. He has an infectious laugh. The anticipation of a surprise makes his eyes twinkle; and I happily anticipate what will happen in a few short minutes, a deep-throated chuckle. Like any infant, he giggles when you tickle his feet or tummy. He is always ready for attention, especially if he feels there might be a big surprise involved. Using a blanket to cover and uncover a stuffed animal or my face is also a favorite. If game rules are simple, he will want to enjoy the activity over and over again. Such games are invaluable as brain stimulators and lessons in basic, human communication.

Just like peek-a-boo, pop-up books or tab stories encourage the very young to interact by using the element of surprise. In *How Many Bugs in a Box?* the author, David A. Carter, has created a special package to open on every page. Inside each is an unexpected delight, one or more funny, original bugs. Because children respond to color, he paints the boxes bright red, blue, yellow and green. He uses *size and shape* words such as tall, small, square and thin that correspond to the visuals, which are noodle bugs or other highly imaginative creatures. The author uses *descriptive* words such as tough, pretty, mellow, hungry, and long to tell about the bugs, the number of which increase by one on each page. Counting becomes part of the fun. The author ends the story by giving the child a directive, "Careful, don't let them out!" When a child like Nicolas sees mellow yellow fish bugs or four fast fleas, he is amused no matter how many times he has shared the book with me. And so am I, at his delight.

This book had been a favorite of Alexander too, when he was two. When he became four, Hank and I began to take him on a few day trips by himself. We always had a not too distant destination in mind such as the wonder-filled A. C. Gilbert Children's Museum in Salem, Oregon, or Multnomah Falls, which has wonderful hiking paths. After we went home to St. Louis after our first special outing, I talked with Alexander on the phone and asked him what he enjoyed the most while grandma and grandpa were visiting. He knew his answer right away. He liked playing catch-me-if-you-can in the backyard. It was not our day trip, as I had expected; and I was a bit disappointed because I had enjoyed it so much. We had played the ancient game of chase and tag outside many times, especially after dinner, collapsing on the lawn in breathless giggles after the intense dodging and running. This proved to me once again that children prefer spontaneous fun while adults lean toward organized activities. Inside the house, when it was cold or rainy during winter visits, we played seek and find to the point of adult exhaustion. Regardless of the season, after chase and run, it was time for a pop-up book like *How Many Bugs in a Box* while I recovered.

SEVENTY-FIVE

Jim

*"Remember how God led you for forty years in the wilderness
...The clothes on your back did not wear out and your feet
were not swollen." (Deuteronomy 8: 2, 4)*

Ruth, Hank, and I took Alexander to Fort Clatsop one gray, foggy summer day. Fort Clatsop is a restoration of the rough-and-ready stockade that Lewis and Clark and their party built on a hillside in what is now Oregon, near the mouth of the Columbia River. There they spent a miserably wet winter with less than one week of sun before turning around and heading back to their starting place, St. Louis. Like many Americans I've long been fascinated by their epic trek, particularly since, like them, I began in St. Louis and ended up in the Northwest, although it took me twenty years to their three to get here via Denver.

I was actually wondering if Alexander was going to find anything to interest him at the reconstructed fort or in the Visitors' Center. There was plenty there for the inquisitive grown-up to enjoy—gadgets to look at, displays and captions to read, even a movie if I recall. But I feared that Alexander would be bored, and then difficult to deal with, without cars or airplanes or dinosaurs. As it happened, he was patient with the adult items and then got interested in the props in the fort—coonskin caps and thin blankets on lower bunk beds. Alexander's grandfather got to chatting with one of the guides about Stephen Ambrose and his book *Undaunted Courage*. Fully in charge of distraction, I lifted Alexander up to see the top bunk of a claustrophobic sleeping niche so he could stroke the furs scattered on it. We went outside and followed the sounds to a weapons demonstration. The guns that these explorers needed for their very survival especially fascinated him.

What he liked best of all, though, was down on the inlet below the Fort. An observation gazebo sat on the water and around it were dugouts, anchored down and stable for climbing in and out of, which we did. I suppose these canoes resembled some of the watercraft that Lewis and Clark rode down from the Rockies to the ocean. We snapped a lot of pictures of Alexander standing in a dugout with each of us. There were no oars to pretend with, but we were on dry land anyway.

When I see those pictures now, what I wish for Alexander are future happy voyages. He was born in this mysteriously beautiful part of the country, amid infinite shadings of gray and green. It had taken Easterners like Lewis and Clark and Midwesterners like me a long, arduous time to get to these places, where stunning beauty drifts in and out of visibility. When Clark finally saw the Pacific, he simply remarked in his journal, "Ocean in sight—oh, the joy!" It gives me joy to think that Alexander *began* his journey of discovery here.

SEVENTY-SIX

Hank

"Life can only be understood backwards, but it must be lived forwards." (Soren Kierkegaard)

The grandsons are home in Vancouver after a visit. The baby bed is back in the basement with the highchair and toys. While I am down there, I locate all of the croquet balls lurking in shadows to be stepped on with disastrous consequences and return them to their proper place. Except for the one that I couldn't find.

I take one last look at the baby bed that has served two generations and recall that Lisa informed us that next time new sleeping arrangements will be necessary because Nicolas is outgrowing it. I remind myself to add mattress sales to the list of things I search for in the newspaper. We will have to go furniture shopping; but not too soon, I hope.

I remember that I expressed an interest in doing mazes with Alexander, and Lisa bought a simple book of them. But I have no idea where the book went, and we never got around to it.

I find the recipe for apple pie that I had tacked to the refrigerator in expectation of making one when we returned from picking apples. We never got around to that either. Oh, well.

I remember that I had promised to take the boys to the carousel before they left. But we had no time!

SECOND HELPINGS

I find the videos that we didn't watch and put them in my car so I will remember to return them to the store.

I find the remains of the cake that I made for their first meal with us. The boys wouldn't eat it because it was too elaborate, and they were full of Aunt Jennifer's chocolate chip cookies anyway. I calculate that this is the second time this has happened and make a mental note to keep it simple next time. The wrinkled cake goes down the disposal, the recipe in the trash.

I find fingerprints on the patio door and try to figure out which grandson they belong to. Easy. Some are much lower than the others.

I remember that we never made it to the library to see if there were any books about bats and knighthood, two current interests.

I re-hang the picture that would have been over Nicolas's bed were it not a severe temptation. I bring vases down from high places, put the fireplace tools back out, and call the piano tuner.

I put away the vaporizer that we have needed on almost every previous visit and am amazed that no one got sick or hurt during our time together.

I look at the unread magazine and newspaper pile, which has grown alarmingly high in the last several days. But mostly I listen to the silence, wish for noise, and try to figure out when the next visit is likely to occur.

SEVENTY-SEVEN

Ruth

"Be generous and you will be prosperous. Help others, and you will be helped." (Proverbs 11.25)

Sometimes when I take my grandsons for a long ride in the car and the restraints begin to frustrate, we listen to music or make up nonsense rhymes. Alexander laughs when he thinks the rhymes are funny. Used to this game, he now chooses an occasional poetry book for bedtime reading without much prompting. *Read-Aloud Rhymes for the Very Young* concentrates on poems that deal with the first words children learn and what they see or feel. Some are nonsensical and others are about wonder. Jack Prelutsky selected the poems. The second highest compliment that a grandparent can receive is when a child asks you to reread a poem. The highest compliment is when comic timing brings about a hearty laugh as the picture a poem paints connects with the words.

In the introduction to this book, Jim Trelease says, "The first sound a child hears is actually a poem—the rhythmic, rhyming beat-beat-beat of a mother's heart. This sets the stage for a natural and lifelong love of rhythm and rhyme."

Nicolas is learning new words at an incredible rate and loves to parrot the words that I say as I read each poem. He can't handle anything too long yet, so poetry is the perfect medium for capturing, and holding, his attention.

One of the fun games all children like to play connects

food or familiar objects to rhyme. In a singsong voice I say, "Alexander likes oats, Alexander likes teas, Alexander likes goats, yes, thank you, please." He shakes his head and then imitates my exaggerated rhythm while changing the silly verse to food preferences that he actually likes to eat like cheese, rice, and chocolate. Then we do the opposite, and he tells me what he dislikes ending with, "No, thank you, please. Sometimes he makes outrageous choices, like worms or, even worse, broccoli, and we laugh.

One of the many, many poems that uses repetition effectively in this book is "The Little Turtle." It repeats in the second stanza, "He snapped at a mosquito. He snapped at a flea. He snapped at a minnow. And he snapped at me." The book is full of wonderful rhymes that give the young child a framework for memorizing verses and increasing vocabulary.

It is not unusual for a child to repeat and repeat the same singsong words that a game has created. If you add a drum or a cooking pot with a spoon to beat time as you say rhythmic words, the child will think it is great fun. He or she will not have to be coaxed to drum away. The beat will not always match your rhyme, but the activity is lots of fun, for as long as you can stand the noise.

SEVENTY-EIGHT

Jim

"If all were written down, the world itself, I suppose, would not hold all the books that would have to be written."
(John 21: 25)

The plot of Roberto Benigni's Academy Award winning film *Life Is Beautiful* centers on a father telling his son a story that saves the son's life. Some people have sharply criticized this movie because the story the father tells is so absurdly far from the reality from which he is shielding his son. Namely, they are prisoners in a German death camp near the end of World War II, which has engulfed the character's family. What struck me, however, was the man's extraordinary unselfishness in ignoring his own fear and despair in his effort to keep things believably comic, and hopeful, for his son.

Should all the stories we tell our children be the truth and nothing but the truth? You be the judge. One hot summer day Hank and Ruth and I took Alexander on a jaunt. We had a late start, choosing a destination got complicated, and time was lost when we stopped for ice cream, so in the end we decided to go to a nearby island that was a little piece of country very near to the city. As it happened, Alexander was then much enamored of a video about a visit to Old McDonald's Farm during which people sang and danced and were both wearyingly active and overacting. When we told him we were going to a farm, he made the connection and asked if it was Old McDonald's. Since he was a little cranky at that moment, I glibly said yes.

The island turned out to be a fabulous place. As we drove around it haphazardly, we saw sheep, a running horse, and we even came across a herd of lumbering cows crossing the road just in front of our car. We found wild blackberries, which we picked for free, and some blueberries and marionberries and corn, which we Paid to Pick. Alexander, an engineer's son, chewed me out for leaving twigs and leaves in with the tiny blueberries.

After a splendid afternoon, we were nearing the bridge to the mainland, when Alexander turned to me suspiciously and said, "This wasn't Old McDonald's Farm, was it?" I was stammering, trying to summon cows and berries to my defense, when a large, rosy-cheeked man, wearing a Caterpillar cap and riding a green John Deere, drove into view. The three adults chorused, "There's Old McDonald!" And God bless the farmer—when we waved and yelled, he waved back, with a slow, sweet, bashful smile spreading across his face.

SEVENTY-NINE

Hank

"The real menace in dealing with a five-year-old is that in no time at all you begin to sound like a five-year-old."
(Jean Kerr)

Like most children, Alexander began speaking with nouns and verbs, mostly English words (chocolate) with occasional French terms (piscine), perfectly accented. Now that he is five, he has added adjectives, correctly used. This shows the growing ability to not only define his surroundings but also to make judgments about them.

He likes to sit on my lap at the computer and diddle with the keyboard. This is, perhaps, not such a good idea because it turns an expensive appliance that has become a necessary tool in my daily life into a toy. But grandfathers have a hard time saying *no*. There is no real discernible harm in the activity, I tell myself. But just in case I close the door.

Not so long ago he held down a key and row upon row of Xs began to fill the screen. "Stop it," I insisted. "Write your name instead," added my ever-hopeful inner teacher.

Xs continued to march across and down the screen.

"Boring," I commented.

Alexander, head bobbing and giggling, managed to keep his finger on the key.

"Boring!" I exclaimed with more heat.

He doubled over in laughter, almost falling from my lap.

It became a daily game. When I thought he was engaged in an activity that didn't involve me, I would stealthily ease into my office to read the e-mail, check investments, or write a bit. Alexander would always find me and the game would continue.

Ruth, on the phone with Lisa in West Palm Beach last week, asked Alexander how church had been that morning.

"Boring!" I heard him call out even though I was reading the paper and was only half-tuned into the conversation.

"But I thought you liked to sing," Ruth protested, trying to elicit a positive response.

"Boring!" I heard Alexander repeat with heat, honestly and accurately nailing his morning experience and sounding a lot like me.

Off the phone Ruth was dismayed. "I wonder where he learned *that* word?" she mused with disapproval for his teacher.

I put the print closer to my eyes as if engrossed in an article and didn't answer. I opted to avoid confession unless further confronted and, bowing to the inevitable, decided that next time I'd introduce him to *tedious* and *monotonous*.

EIGHTY

RUTH

"Intelligent people are always eager and ready to learn."
(Proverbs 18.15)

 These thoughts are being composed on the computer. They are saved regularly, edited, saved again, printed, read, and then changed again. I know the meaning of *hard drive* and how to use the mouse, the keyboard, software, and programs such as Microsoft Word to accomplish my goals. I couldn't make it through the day without checking my e-mail and responding. Our *Trash* has to be emptied more often than just a few months ago. I couldn't work without computer skills either since my job routinely requires me to both teach and use computers. There is a long list of new vocabulary words that have crept into my conversation over the past few years. Still, technological advances make my head spin. It wasn't too many years ago, in the Stone Age, when Hank and I were trying to decide if we needed a second television set in our bedroom to watch three channels.
 Alexander knows most of the computer words I know too, but his programs are more specialized. In fact, along with fun games and basic skill activities he is also learning many words and entire programs in French. A new computer, a Christmas gift from four grandparents, is upstairs for Alexander to use while his parents keep their finances, flight scheduling

software, recipes, e-mail, adult games, and the Internet on another computer downstairs. Along with new technology, new problems are created. Marc Brown speaks to this in *Arthur's Computer Disaster*. Mom tells Arthur not to touch her computer while she is gone. Arthur loads *Deep Dark Secret* anyway. Arthur and Buster start fighting over the mouse, and the computer crashes to the floor. Mom is on her way home and Arthur just doesn't know what to do. He calls on his friend Brain to fix the problem but with little success. Mother arrives and after dinner she decides to use her computer. In a state of panic Arthur confesses all, and Mom fixes the problem with a simple adjustment to the switch.

Understanding computers and how to use them is a must in both public and private schools these days. Children in the lower grades at my school learn to save their work to the desktop, and they are taught word processing skills like the Herzog Method at an early age. Being able to use the Internet for research has rapidly become a critically important skill.

Many experts warn that being on a computer is an isolating activity. It need not be. Sharing Alexander's computer games and other programs with him has provided lots of quality time for us. He says, "Grandma, did you see that?" in reference to images floating by on the screen. Keeping up with the world our grandsons will live in continues to challenge me and keep me growing as well.

EIGHTY-ONE

JIM

"The wolf lives with the lamb, the panther lies down with the kid, calf and lion cub feed together with a little boy to lead them. . . .They do no hurt, no harm, on all my holy mountain." (Isaiah 11: 6, 9)

Alexander has watched a lot of TV and videotapes in his time. His parents carefully monitor what goes in, but this is, after all, maybe above all, a media age. When he was only eighteen months old, he was already a big fan of the witty British animation series about the dotty inventor Wallace and his long-suffering, intelligent dog Gromit. And, like many American children these days, he has amassed a considerable video library of Disney and Daffy Duck classics and the works of other notable animators. His designated drawer is overflowing with cassettes and not just in English but also in the French of his father's side, which he has heard and understood from the start. He doesn't just watch cartoons, of course; in addition to the favored "Arthur" on PBS, he also watches all the live-action shows, from Teletubbies early on, through his Barney phase, and then, in pre-school mode, moving on to Sesame Street and more sophisticated fare.

But—and this is the point—this is all that his parents let him watch. He doesn't get to view the cartoons on the network and cable shows, neither the crude ones for adults nor the violent ones targeted to kids. This, of course, has not spared him some of the painful facts of life. When he was not much more than three, he already knew to fast-forward Bambi—in English or in French—past the off-camera shooting of Bambi's mother if he didn't want to deal with sadness or fear. And he very early got a look at stylish crime when he watched Feathers McGraw in *The Wrong Trousers* try to steal a diamond, only to be thwarted by the plucky Gromit.

But he must have missed the flashy violence that a lot of American children see so often that they don't even register it. When we finally took him, on Christmas Day, to see his first outside-the-home movie, *A Bug's Life*, he couldn't handle it. Some of it was the cruelly loud soundtrack; the mini-theater's speakers were meant for a far larger space. But it was also the (bloodless) mayhem and the menacing Bad Bugs, parodies for adults, but too real for him. I'm told that pretty early in the film he turned to his mom and said, "I'm just a little boy (he was five plus change); this is too scary for me." Still he tried to soldier on, but in the end we had to leave a bit before the final scene, which was fairly predictable in any case.

On balance I'm glad we left, though, and glad that, in a world where children get anesthetized to violence early, Alexander can still be clear that there are some things that are too much for little kids—not just too much to experience, but even too much to watch. My prayer is that this could somehow be more and more true for more and more kids.

EIGHTY-TWO

Hank

"I had just put my young son to bed for the umpteenth time and my patience was worn thin. When I heard him cry, 'Mama' again, I yelled at him, 'if you call 'Mama' one more time, I'll spank you!' After that there was quiet. Then just as I sat down, I heard a wee whisper, 'Mrs. Green, may I have a drink?'" (Jean Green)

When Alexander was very small, I would often baby sit in the afternoon so that Lisa, who seldom had the opportunity, and Ruth, who wisely appreciated advice other than mine in selecting clothes, could shop. These expeditions often became marathons, and I didn't mind in the least. However, I will admit that putting Ali down for his nap after lunch was the best part of the experience. I would dig into the newspapers, books, or magazines that had piled up during the always activity filled visits and pray that he would sleep for hours. The feeling never lasted though. I would begin to count the few short hours we had left together and be ready to play again. If the nap approached two hours, I would worry. Was he all right? Was he even breathing? I would invariably go in and wake him up, and he would cry for more sleep.

We went to Rockwood Reservation for a class on colors in nature. Halfway up the trail and trying to find black objects in the woods as instructed, Ali became very quiet. I thought he was bored with our assigned task or maybe frightened. Back under the pavilion the eager, young guide fed us cookies and brought out a snake. All of the other children went over to touch it, but Ali refused to participate, had a major hissy fit, and fell into a deep sleep with his head on a picnic table. He did not awaken when I carried him to the car, drove home, and put him in his bed. When I expressed concern, Lisa analyzed the time before we had left. Ali had coughed a lot during the night and had had only five hours of sleep. "Dimetapp," she concluded.

We were entertaining two elderly friends during Lisa's visit. Not used to being around active, noisy children, they were clearly not enjoying the company of a two-year old. We waited until after his bedtime to begin serving, but the dinner did not go well. Ali would not settle down. His one desire was to be where we were. He cried. And cried. Our guests left early.

We went to the neighborhood park. After play, we sat on a bench and watched planes fly over. Ali, huddled under my protective arm, became very quiet. I looked down and discovered that he had fallen into a deep sleep. I could not wake him. With no alternative, I carried him a mile or more home. Refreshed from his nap, Alexander was ready to play while I, not as young as I used to be, seriously needed to recover from the ordeal.

There seems to be a natural law that causes children to fall asleep when you don't want them to and keeps them awake when you want them to fall asleep.

EIGHTY-THREE

Ruth

"Books are the quietest and most constant of friends, they are the most accessible and wisest of counselors, and the most patient of teachers." (Charles W. Eliot)

When Alexander was born, three generations of relatives were overjoyed. Gifts were sent from far and near to welcome this newborn into the world. A package arrived from France. Inside was a sterling silver place setting containing a bowl, a small cup, a napkin holder, and a toddler's spoon and fork. A traditional baptismal necklace and bracelet were sent as well. This jewelry is to be worn by both males and females until they are teenagers. The relatives in the United States sent money, clothes, a quilted blanket with nursery rhymes lovingly stitched onto it, a CD containing lullabies, and a subscription to *Baby Bug*, a toddler magazine.

Alexander was our first grandchild, so we were especially anxious to find meaningful gifts that would endure the passage of time. Toys and clothes are invariably temporary, and we gave lots of both, but nothing stuck until I found a treasure called *Corduroy* by Don Freeman. A stuffed Corduroy and a charming, serene video came with the book.

Corduroy is a cute little bear with green overalls who is overlooked again and again by customers in the department store, where he lives on a shelf. He has an adventure during which he loses a button. In the story Corduroy makes both good and bad choices, like knocking a lamp over. Happiness is assured when the little girl who wants him gets money from her piggy bank and returns to purchase him. Another delightful book with the same character is called *A Pocket for Corduroy*. Alexander has had his friend for almost five years now. Corduroy always goes to bed with him. Assorted other stuffed friends change nightly. Beanie Babies faded and Pokeman paled, but Corduroy continues to be the sleep mate of first choice.

Sometimes Alexander delays bedtime by hiding Corduroy. Grandma and grandpa go on a big search to solve the problem of the missing bear. Pretending to be distraught, we look in his favorite hiding places. Alexander does not participate in the search because he knows exactly where Corduroy is. Were he really gone for good, there would be tears. With some coaching from the owner himself, Corduroy always turns up. This game gives Alexander at least another ten minutes.

EIGHTY-FOUR

JIM

"If anyone has two coats they must share with the one who has none." (Luke 3: 11)

Like many children, Alexander has always had plenty of stuffed animals. The first present I gave him, if I remember the sequence, was a stuffed bear with a red T-shirt which read, "Someone at Seattle University [where I teach] Loves You Very Much." It now lounges idly among fifty or so other, mostly ignored, cute and cuddly friends in Alexander's bookcase upstairs awaiting an audition for Toy Story III. Candidly, I have to admit that it is not his favorite animal. That honor goes to Corduroy Bear, perhaps because, unlike the Seattle University bear, Corduroy, media star, came with a videotape.

Alexander needs some of his animals when it's time for bed. He hates to fall asleep and miss things, like the adult conversation, music, or TV program wafting through his door. He also, as I've mentioned elsewhere, hates just as much to wake up.

One afternoon, when he was just beginning to talk, he was fussing about going down for a nap, so I offered to stay in the darkened room with him. Ears cocked, I stretched out on the rug next to his crib. There was a ruminative pause during which I could hear him slowly sucking on his pacifier. Then I heard him climb up on the side of his crib so he could look down and check to see if I had moved. No fool, he correctly surmised that I would probably sneak out as soon as he was asleep. But of course I was still there, so he lay down again.

After another ruminative pause, I heard from above me, "Want a bear?" He had noticed that I was lying down solo, and, little as he was, wanted to be generous to the less endowed.

"Sure," I replied and a panda, but not Corduroy, thudded softly against my shoulder.

I took this as just one of the many signs that even very small children have the kind of beautiful human traits that seem to come straight from a loving God.

EIGHTY-FIVE

Hank

"Son, when you stop learning, you will soon neglect what you already know." (Proverbs 19.27)

Nicolas constantly shocks and amazes me.

Not yet two, he was busily using Magic Markers to make a white piece of paper disappear under a series of haphazard, multi-hued lines. "I think I'll use purple," I said aloud to myself about my own drawing, an only slightly more mature design than Nicolas's.

"Purple," Nicolas repeated with perfect enunciation.

We played chase around an area rug with a white border in the front hall. "I'm going to get you!" I announced each time I neared, ready to grab him up and smother him with hugs just before he lost his balance. But I became winded and slowed down. "I'm gonna get chew," I heard Nicolas say with considerable determination just before he grabbed my legs from behind.

I offered him a cookie, and he said, "Thank you." I was, proudly, the first human being to hear him utter this important phrase, hard evidence that civilizing is well underway. I could hardly wait to tell his parents, and I hoped that I was at least partially responsible for this bit of learning.

But the scene from his recent visit that plays most often on the screen in my memory is of Nicolas scrambling onto the piano stool, sitting with his back perfectly erect, and positioning his fingers just above the white keys as if awaiting the opening notes of the concerto. Then he delicately played a series of discordant notes as if he, self-assured about his talent, was auditioning for Julliard. When the notes died away he pointed to the music book on the piano rack and grunted purposefully. That was my signal to turn the page and discuss the next piece. Because of his age, he seldom completed more than two numbers before dropping from the bench to engage in another two-minute activity.

How did he learn to imitate Andras Schiff and say *purple*? The answer is both simple and complex. His mother has been taking him to Kindermusik classes, which he loves. He is exposed to singing, instrumentation, and structure at each lesson. Learning accumulates. Also, like any child he imitates what he sees and hears, so the adults with whom he has contact had better be appropriate role models.

I renewed my vow to withhold petty judgments, avoid demeaning gossip, watch my language, and control my temper while around Nicolas. You see, we are both into learning, if at different stages.

EIGHTY-SIX

RUTH

"A problem is a chance for you to do your best." (Duke Ellington)

H. A. Rey knows how eager most children are to learn how to ride a bike. In *Curious George Rides a Bike* a delightfully curious but easily distracted monkey is given his first one. He learns very quickly how to ride and decides to help out with a newspaper delivery. He passes a swiftly flowing river. He wonders if a boat made from one of the newspapers would float down that river. His creation drifts away successfully. Taking newspapers from his bag, George begins to make many boats. He jumps on his bike to accompany his fleet and soon hits a rock because he is not paying attention. George flies off his seat. Luckily he is not hurt. However, his tire is bent, and he begins to cry. An attempt to ride the bike with the front wheel up in the air fails. George tires quickly. His curiosity continues to get him in and out of trouble throughout the rest of the story. His owner, the man with the yellow hat, finally finds George.

Alexander was very eager to learn how to ride a bike. Most of the kids in the neighborhood are much older than he and are already very proficient on bikes. His parents told Alexander that he must wear a helmet and kneepads and that during practice the bike would need training wheels. He was afraid of falls, so he did not protest the training wheels, but he did not want to wear a helmet because the other kids on the block made fun of him when he wore one. There was no choice in the matter. Within a few months Alexander, after some spills and scrapes, learned riding technique. Now he has asked for the training wheels to be taken off. His concentration and skill at handling a bike have prepared him for the next step.

When we talked about bike riding on the phone, I could tell he was very proud of his accomplishment. He told me about the teasing from the big kids, but Alexander was feeling successful so it had ceased to bother him. Since most of the neighborhood children like to enjoy the playground equipment in the backyard, they have stopped taunting their host. They now basically get along quite well together.

After one terrible spill, he refused to ride his bike until I visited and re-taught starting and stopping techniques. I tried very hard not to say, "Be careful," each time he lurched forward and gained momentum.

These events in Alexander's life have been about dealing with ridicule, being willing to make mistakes, re-gaining self-confidence, and developing the power to concentrate in order to learn a new skill. At a very young age children must learn to be risk takers while dealing with warnings and criticism, so grandparents, like the man in the yellow hat, must listen, praise, and foster independence.

EIGHTY-SEVEN

JIM

"For who has known the mind of the Lord, or who has been God's counselor?" (First Corinthians 2:16, quoting Isaiah 40:13)

In his cordial book *The Zen of Recovery*, Mel Ash repeatedly points out that the goal of Zen meditation is to return as often as one can to Beginner's Mind, to Don't Know mind. This kind of mind can enable a person to approach a particular moment or a particular situation with an openness to its possibilities. This kind of mind keeps us from wasting opportunities we might otherwise lose because of our fears and our dislikes.

Children often have this kind of fresh attitude, and in this, as in so many other areas, our grandchildren can be spiritual teachers to an older generation whose fears and dislikes are more than likely etched in stone. Alexander has an endearing quirk that sounds like this feature of Zen, and he puts it into a form that also recalls Zen and its koans, paradoxical and contradictory riddles. When you ask Alexander something, like, "Do you know what that big green machine over there is?" or "Do you know how to turn on the VCR?" he invariably replies, brimming with self-confidence, "Yes!" But if you follow up by asking, "O.K., what is it?" or "How do you turn it on?" he replies, just as cheerfully, "I don't know!"

SECOND HELPINGS

Who knows what's going on in a grandchild's head, or how they reconcile contradictions like these—if indeed they bother about them at all. Maybe Alexander's joyous "I don't know!" attests to his willingness to hear the answers all over again, just as he is perfectly willing to listen to the same Curious George story for the twentieth night in a row. Or maybe he senses one of the great spiritual truths: a lot of the most important things we both know and Don't Know, at least with a knowledge we can put into words. We should never lose our capability of being pleasantly surprised by the familiar.

EIGHTY-EIGHT

Hank

"Never ask, 'Oh, why were things so much better in the old days?' It's not an intelligent question." (Ecclesiastes 7.10)

According to psychologist Sylvia Rimm, author of *See Jane Win*, family travel provides opportunities for adventure and family bonding that bode success for children later in life. I couldn't agree more.

I love to travel. So does Ruth. Because we were teachers with a lot of the summer off, we were able to take long trips with our children during which we explored every inch of North America that was accessible by car. I have a vivid memory of Matt, who ate too many pancakes at breakfast, throwing up in the back seat halfway up an isolated canyon in Arizona. I recall climbing through a porthole seconds before departure after I discovered that Matt and I were on the wrong boat and about to depart on a seventeen hour trip to Newfoundland. I remember getting stuck halfway down a tube slide on a playground in Monterey, California. We had some bad experiences too.

Ruth and I would love to do it all a second time by taking our grandsons to places we loved but have not seen for years, but that is expecting too much. It would take the boys away from their parents for long stretches of time and rob them of family travel opportunities and experiences we so enjoyed.

As a result we are content to take Alexander, and later

Nicolas when he is a bit older, on day trips that are quite different from but no less delightful than the vacations we used to take.

One recent summer day Ruth and I took Alexander up the Columbia Gorge to Goldendale, Washington. We left early in the morning with the plan to stop whenever he wanted to explore something by the roadside. As a result we stopped to discuss an accident marker in the form of a white cross that was covered with flowers on a high promontory. We stopped for seasonal berries, homemade jelly, and candy at a roadside stand. We honked and shouted in tunnels, strolled by the river and kicked rocks, watched windsurfers dip and sway, waved as a train went by, introduced a new generation to some unusual sculpture, painting, and decorative arts at the Maryhill Museum. We ate chocolate chip cookies that were not a reward for consuming vegetables but a reward in themselves as we peered at a cascading waterfall. We had a fine time and were home for dinner.

Every time we anticipate being with our grandsons we have an idea in mind of where to take them by ourselves. If we get to have a memorable day like the one above, we are happy. If their parents reject the idea, we understand. But we never give up the hope for a *next time*.

EIGHTY-NINE

Ruth

"Emotion drives attention and attention drives learning and memory." (Susan Kovalik and Karen D. Olsen)

During a winter vacation from school, Hank and I went to visit. The weather was awful. An ice storm closed the airport and caused power outages. We had lots of indoor time to fill.

Alexander, who has always loved fantasy, was four years old then. We went upstairs and sat on his bed together. Already having read it many times on previous occasions, we decided to revisit *Three Little Bears*. Alexander gathered up three stuffed bears that he had under his bed and in his bookcase and lined them up on the pillows by size. As the reading progressed, I found myself acting out the story. I, no longer Grandma, became Goldilocks.

In the first retelling Alexander played the Papa Bear. He coarsened his voice to fit the character. He stomped about his bedroom, and his facial expressions were appropriately gruff. Still Goldilocks, I answered his question about sleeping in his bed in a high pitched, tremulous voice. He was pleased with both performances.

In the second retelling, Alexander decided to become the baby bear. This time he made himself physically small and sounded just like a cub. I asked him to try to be Goldilocks on the third retelling. He didn't want to do it at first, but I put

SECOND HELPINGS

a blanket around his shoulders and tied a towel around his head. He enjoyed the sound of his own voice, and we were both so tickled by his performance that we broke out in laughter.

In the fall Lisa told me on the phone that Alexander had volunteered to be Papa Bear in a performance at his preschool. His best friend Jack was Baby Bear.

Abuela, by Arthur Dorros, is a wonderful book about a Spanish grandma and grandchild going on imaginary adventures together. They fly in the air and see many sights. Since each story must be told through the mind's eye, the participants are given an opportunity to use rich language with descriptions, feelings, tone, and mood development. Spanish words are used throughout the story with the English translation making it a fun bilingual book to share.

Every time we visit now, Alexander wants to go on another adventure with me. That's just one of the things he loves about his Abuela. She likes adventures too!

NINETY

Jim

"In every land, by every tongue, / Let the Creator's name be sung." (Old 100, Thomas Ken)

My sister-in-law has taught children from France, Congo, Russia, Iran, and Japan in the past few years. And as I've mentioned elsewhere, not so unusual in our culture anymore, my grandnephews are bilingual. Well, sort of.

Soon to start kindergarten, Alexander understands the French spoken by his papa and his papa's side of the family perfectly well. But he doesn't often speak French, at least not with the English-speaking part of the family. Of course, we English speakers sprinkle our conversations with French words and phrases, so both sides are mixing linguistically, just as we mixed genetically in the boys.

I'm not sure Alexander quite got the difference when he was a bit younger. He used to fall back on French for some of the more common things in his world. When he was just learning to talk, I think I heard him say, *"Regarde!"* (Look!) one day to his French grandmother at the foot of the stairs. And he has consistently preferred "monsieur" to "man."

Nicolas never passes a piscine (swimming pool) without bringing it to everyone's attention, and he has clearly chosen the French pronunciation for his brother's name, calling him *Ah lay zand*.

Around the age of four Alexander began to discern a

pattern in who said which words for what. One day I said, "*Voila!*" when I found a missing dinosaur in the bottom of the toy box, and he gave me the sort of fishy stare he reserves for peculiar adult behavior. "You're talking French like papa!" summed up the infraction.

After years of taking Latin—I was formed for the priesthood in part in the old school—I found it easy to teach myself to read French, back in the seminary. But I've never learned to hear or speak or write it very well. Sometimes when I'm with Alexander's French relations, I wish I could get them to write down what they've just said so I can get it. I do all right with most nouns, and even some adjectives (like '*joli*," "cute," which I've heard around Alexander a lot). But the verbs, which change a lot more in French than in English, baffle me. Anyway, I'm looking forward to the day, a few years in the future, when Nicolas, who is rapidly following in Alexander's linguistic footsteps, catches up. I can just imagine them dropping into French with each other when they want to ease Uncle Jim out of the conversation. The delight will more than make up for the bafflement.

NINETY-ONE

Hank

"Sorrow is better than laughter; it may sadden your face, but it sharpens your understanding." (Ecclesiastes 7.4)

We had spent six days together at our house in St. Louis and an additional week in Florida. In Saint Louis I noted a new independent streak in Alexander. When I took him to the playground, he did not need, or want, constant supervision. He easily made a friend, and each time I looked up from my newspaper they were running together. I could hear Ali proclaiming, "I'm Batman and you're Robin!" In the entire hour he didn't come over even one time to be assured that I was still there or to ask for me to swing him. I had to approach him with the news that it was time to go, and he protested.

In Florida he wore water wings in the pool and showed a fearlessness that I found both impressive and alarming. He ducked his head under water, attempted an unassisted float, and duck paddled into the deep end. Fiercely proud, he pushed my hand away repeatedly because he was trying to show me what he could do.

Otherwise, he still took my hand to skip and to negotiate busy parking lots, gave up on long board games with complex rules, and wanted his usual complement of roughhousing. I was Joker to his Batman on many occasions and was always vanquished by the flashlight, which magically produced a laser beam when he needed one to fend me off.

SECOND HELPINGS

It was now almost six a.m. Our plane from West Palm Beach to St. Louis was to take off in two hours. For the last week Ruth and I had shared a bedroom with Alexander, and it was about this time each morning when he would come bounding into bed between us for a hug and perhaps a tussle before we headed for the coffee maker and the orange juice. But this was the final morning. I was dressed and ready to leave. My suitcase, packed the night before, was in the hall by the door. I passed Alexander's bed for the final time. He was still sleeping. His head, with dark hair against the pillow, was turned toward the wall. I could barely see his face in the dim light. I had a sudden urge to reach down and stroke his hair. But to do that would certainly awaken him.

I could not take that risk because, then, I would have to actually say goodbye. That would cause sadness for both of us. I recalled his saying, "One day, Grandma, just one day!" to Ruth as he protested our quick passage through Vancouver on our way to Alaska last summer. Good-byes, even temporary ones, are still difficult; so I contented myself with just one last look and a quick prayer that he would continue to grow well and take risks under the protection of Divine Providence since I would not always be there to grab him should he drift into the deep end before he is ready.

Ninety-Two

Ruth

"Reading books in one's youth is like looking at the moon through a crevice; reading books in middle age is like looking at the moon in one's courtyard; and reading books in old age is like looking at the moon on an open terrace. This is because the depth of benefits of reading varies in proportion to the depth of one's own experience." (Chang Ch'ao)

The routine of preparing for bed by taking a bath, brushing teeth, combing hair, or, if the child is very young, taking a bottle, sets the tone for completing the day. It's a very good idea to make bedtime reading a part of the ritual. It can easily become a favorite pastime for young children and, hopefully, a habit. It is much more than just another shared activity, though. It's a way for both caregiver and child to relax, to cuddle with each other, to hear a good story about a familiar character or someone new, and to ease the child into sleep.

Nicolas did not suck his thumb or use a pacifier, but he found a bottle of warm milk very comforting at the end of the day. He also could relate to and had a special affection for the stuffed bunny in the story *The Runaway Bunny* written by Margaret Wise Brown. In this story, which I read to him almost every night, the little bunny wants to run away. The mother reassures him that she will run after him, "for you are my little bunny." The loving mother is always supportive in the story regardless of what adventure her offspring wants to pursue. A message of security reassures young children. As Nicolas settled down for the night in his bed, he clutched his stuffed bunny under one arm; and his body language said that all was well with him.

Each time I saw this, it became for me that glorious moment when the caregiver knows that another day has been completed, and now one can steal some quiet time with a cup of tea, a phone call, a TV show, or a good book. I would proceed accordingly.

Lisa came to visit with the boys. She spent the last morning packing, a major undertaking considering the seemingly endless number of items needed for young children. In a small carry on bag that she would not check were stowed the last minute objects, invaluable treasures that she could not live without, not even for one night if a layover became necessary or their luggage was delayed. As she reviewed the assortment of bottles, snacks, diapers, a change of clothing, she noticed that Nicolas' bunny was missing. She simply could not leave without it! The plane could go without her. Before an all out house search commenced, I found the bunny, which had fallen behind the bed. Hugging the lost animal, Lisa's face changed from stress to calm and I remembered her *ba*, a blanket that she reduced to shreds when she was her son's age. She would stroke it as I read, time after time, *The Curious Cow*.

NINETY-THREE

Jim

"For I was sick and you visited me." (Matthew 25:36)

    I have a close friend who lives in the same city as Alexander. The friend, a member of Alcoholics Anonymous, goes by the sobriquet "Harry the Clown." Clowning—with the traditional wild wig and big shoes, not just freelance fooling around—is his chief hobby. At one point, Harry had a bad bout of health involving some heart problems. Around that time, I was driving around town with Alexander and told him that later that day I was going to see my friend the Clown, and that he was sick.

    Alexander, who was three, became very concerned and catechized me about Harry's illness. "Your friend the clown—he's sick?"

"Yes, he is."

He thought this over. "Is he at home?"

"Yep."

"Is he crying?" I inwardly chuckled at this but kept a somber expression on my face and said *yes*, only to learn later from Harry that he actually had been doing some crying because his illness had him badly scared.

    And then Alexander said something which, as happens from time to time, made my eyes burn: "I pray for him!"

    Because faith in addition to words also shows itself in deeds, as soon as he returned home, Alexander made a get-well painting for Harry, a watercolor from Alexander's Mark Rothko phase.

I thought of my Jesuit friend, Charley Shelton, and his belief that the basis of all human ethical behavior is empathy. And I sent up a silent prayer of thanks because, even at three, Alexander was well begun on the human ethical path.

NINETY-FOUR

Hank

"Life, for most of us, is a continuous process of getting used to things we hadn't expected." (unknown)

We took Alexander to Tilles Park for the Christmas lights. Five adults plus one baby were cramped in the too warm car, and we had a long wait to get in. But as we drove slowly around the loop and pointed to the displays, Alexander, just barely old enough to be aware, oohed and aahed. We sang Christmas carols. I noted later in my diary, "It was fun, due to him."

In Chicago, my cousin Tom invited us up to his luxurious condo. I oohed and aahed at the expensive décor, the magnificent view of Lake Michigan, and the vertically lighted downtown through a wall of glass and to the right. It was evening, past Alexander's bedtime, and he was getting cranky. Not used to having children around, Tom handed Alexander a golf ball to play with. We left before adult conversation or a disaster could occur. It was not fun, due to him.

We sensed it was a bad idea because he was so young, and we were prepared to leave at the first hint of trouble. But to our amazement, Alexander loved the circus. Too enchanted to sit, he stood in place before his seat transfixed by the high wire acts, the clowns, and the animals. Turning to see if we were clapping too, he applauded each act. It was a magical experience, due to him.

SECOND HELPINGS

We took the Alaska Railroad from Fairbanks to Anchorage. The tickets were very expensive, but how many times in life can you expect to have such a glorious experience and see scenery that awesome? Alas, I saw little of it because for twelve hours I chased an almost two-year old from one end of the train to the other. It was an unpleasant experience...because of him.

I was invited to Play Park's Halloween Party. Ali was a clown. His friend Jack, who is tiny and timid, was, incredibly, Batman. We fished for prizes with a magnet attached to a pole. There was face painting. We stuffed our mouths with cupcakes. It was a wonderful experience because of them.

We were in the Salt Lake City Terminal. The plane was already several hours late when we found out why. Two idiots in Arizona, where our flight was to originate, had made a joke about a bomb on board. It took hours to check every inch of the plane, just in case. We took off at eleven and didn't arrive back in Portland until 12:30 a.m. The last flight to Seattle had taken off, so there was no way for Stan to get to work unless someone drove him there. That six-hour drive wasn't as bad as the six hours we spent in the Terminal. Have you ever spent that much time with a two-year old in a crowded space full of short tempers with nothing to do? It is *not* a wonderful experience.

Both parents and grandparents want to include children in activities and experiences, but each incurs a risk, like Russian Roulette. Optimistic going in, euphoric or despondent going out. You never know.

NINETY-FIVE

Ruth

"One loyal friend is worth ten thousand relatives."
(Euripides)

Friendship is a mystery.

Alexander had come with his parents to visit us for nine days, and it was time to leave. As we got out of the car at the airport, he reached for my hand and said, "I love you Grandma. I really like to come to your house, but I have to go see Jack." Jack has been Alexander's special friend since both boys were five months old. Alexander began this friendship when Lisa would walk to a neighborhood park to meet other moms with young children. It was a great time to share ideas with other new mothers and, perhaps more importantly, get out of the house for a while.

What is it that causes such a bond at so young an age? Why do some childhood friends, despite different paths taken, become lifelong companions while others drift away?

There are visible clues with Jack and Ali. The boys are both athletic, love fantasy, and enjoy playing dinosaurs and cars together. Their opposite personalities somehow balance the relationship.

Arnold Lobel tells about special friendships in two books titled *Frog and Toad Together* and *Days With Frog and Toad*. Toad loses his list of things to do, and Frog helps him solve the problem. Toad wants his seeds to grow immediately. Frog teaches him patience. When Toad has a special treat of cookies, he wants to share his treasures with Toad. Reading adventure books together, Frog and Toad wonder if they are brave. In a humorous way the writer explores the meaning of bravery.

On the first day back home, Alexander was off to the summer zoo program with Jack. Lisa told me over the phone that, after a quick "Hi" and a hug, they were busy playing dinosaurs in the back seat of the car. They joined their assigned class and were off to see a penguin. The zookeeper brought the Antarctic bird closer to the children so that they could learn to identify its body parts. They watched, amazed, as a duck eliminated. Jack and Alexander giggled together. Later, he was eager to report to me on the telephone that the duck made droppings on the paper.

Sampling life in both real experiences and play helps friendships to grow. Now approaching five years of age, Alexander still feels Jack is his number one friend even though Jack has moved to Colorado Springs. The friendship might naturally fade due to distance, but I suspect it won't.

NINETY-SIX

JIM

"The good earth everywhere blooms into spring and greens anew!
Everywhere and forever blue lights the distance! Forever.
.. Forever." ("The Farewell," from The Song of the Earth,
Gustav Mahler and Hans Bethge)

I'm a classical music freak. One of my favorite pieces, or favorite moments in a work, comes at the end of Mahler's cycle of songs for voice and orchestra called *The Song of the Earth*. Near the end of his life and knowingly suffering from the heart disease that would kill him at the age of fifty-one, Mahler found some German translations of Chinese poetry that expressed the state of his soul. The last of the six songs, "The Farewell," is as long as the other five put together. The farewell it depicts is between two old friends. One is being forced to go far away by the hostility and incomprehension of other people.

At the very end Mahler went beyond his Chinese-German text and wrote his own words, at the moment when the two friends actually part, with the traveler heading out into an endless, beautiful blue horizon. The last word, repeated softly over a hushed orchestral shimmer, is "Ewig"—"forever." This is the music that plays in my head when I reflect on the fact that life is quite often a matter of farewells, accompanied by protestations that "we'll keep in touch" that "we" know will not be realized.

This comes to mind now because Alexander is about to experience one of his first real "farewells." Jack, his best friend practically from the day they could both walk, talk, and meet people, is moving with his family to another state, more than a thousand miles away. Even though Alexander may fly to visit his friend from time to time, their special relationship, with Alexander always the larger, more protective of the two, will surely change. I doubt that brief visits will fill the gap. I also suspect that now would not be a good time to point out that Alexander could transfer his big-brotherly feelings to his biological little brother. Maybe this is just another sad lesson in his education in the real world that we all must experience, like the evil Smog Monster in the book that Alexander, given the freedom to make his own selection, has recently met.

"Parting is all we know of heaven / And all we need of hell." (Emily Dickinson)

NINETY-SEVEN

Hank

"Happiness is having a large, loving, caring family in another city." (George Burns)

Two important events occurred this week on consecutive days. The United States Supreme Court began a consideration of grandparents' visitation rights and Alexander had a birthday. The Supreme Court will review cases where grandparents have been denied access to their grandchildren. I know that circumstances change, relationships end, and parents need to exercise control over the adults with whom their children have contact. When divorce or separation occurs, forces take sides and everyone wants control. Hoping to support and advise, the parents of the splitting couple might interfere instead. I realize that it is impossible for outsiders, like judges, to determine where the truth lies when things get so emotional and polarized, but to deny visitation to grandparents is cruel. Inhuman! Before you throw the book at me, realize that I know that they may have been part of the problem. I grant that in some rare cases physical and/or emotional abuse have occurred. Then denial of access makes sense. But we all know that involved parties exaggerate and twist the truth. In any event, judges need superhuman wisdom to decide whose rights should prevail, and I do not envy their position.

Nor do I want to be in the position of the disenfranchised

grandparent. The thought of not being allowed to be a part of my grandsons' lives is too awful to contemplate. If I thought I would never see them again, there would be a giant hole in my life too big to fill with a second career, volunteer work, friends, or travel.

We have never been with Alexander on his birthday. Ruth is still working, and autumn is an impossible time for her to go anywhere. It isn't impossible for me, but I would feel selfish if I were to attend his celebration when she could not. We are certainly not deprived. We take Christmas and summer trips to Vancouver, and Lisa brings the boys to us in the autumn and spring.

But these never really seem enough. I am always sated after a visit and glad to have some time to rest. It takes about two weeks for the memory to fade just enough for me not to be able to instantly conjure a mental picture of either grandson. I begin to wonder if they have a new skill. After a month there is a longing, indeed, a need to touch them. A phone conversation, never ideal with a child anyway, won't satisfy. It is not easy being far away from grandchildren when an occasion that is important to them occurs—the first day of school, a first fishing experience, a childhood illness.

Ruth and I often discuss moving closer to our grandsons. The positive side of this would be more frequent contact. The negative side of this would be more frequent contact. It would have been a joy today to watch Alexander jump on the inflated dragon that was rented for his party, to applaud when he blew out five candles on his cake, and to receive a warm hug for the toys I gave him. But then, if I lived nearby, I would have gone home. When he visits next week, I will have him to myself all day, every day for two weeks. Then *he* will go home.

NINETY-EIGHT

Ruth

"A photograph is a portrait painted by the sun." (Dupins)

At very early ages Alexander and Nicolas have traveled many miles in the air to visit distant relatives and been exposed to other cultures. Maybe it is because their father is a pilot, or maybe it is because their mother loves new adventures, or maybe it is because both sets of grandparents have a thirst to experience the sights around the world and indulge in frequent travel. Studying maps, telling of trips, relating future plans, and the sharing of photos and videos are always a part of any visit together. Everywhere we go, whether together or individually, we send postcards, pick up travel brochures for friends and family, and keep a diary of events. We also cannot resist any souvenirs which might entertain or educate our grandsons.

We always review our trips with Alexander and Nicolas by showing them pre-selected pictures and talking about the sights we have seen that would be of interest to children. When we take either child on an outing, we always attempt to validate the experience with photos not only to remind us of small details that might otherwise be forgotten but also to provide a living legacy, evidence to leave behind.

The boys learn about distant and rarely visited relatives in France and New Caledonia by seeing their pictures. They also see that not all parts of the world nor people look the same.

In other words, families create their own living books that are just as important as published works. For example, when a family collects pictures and organizes them into a photo album about an important event, like a wedding or a graduation, they are creating a very personal nonfiction book. Each family has a different, as in totally unique, story to tell.

Daddy and Me is a picture-story book organized by the late Arthur Ashe and written by his wife Jeanne Moutoussamy-Ashe for their daughter Camera. It is a book of family photos and personal observations that Arthur, who knew he was dying, shares with his daughter. Details recorded in the photographs are to help Camera remember her father.

Photos help young children to sort out feelings. They see different expressions on faces in an album and they begin to relate those expressions to specific emotions. They gain insight into the personalities of family members. They hear family lore. They see the difference between young and old, thin and heavy, tall and short.

Becoming a traveling storyteller with photos and gifts for your grandchild enhances their experience and broadens their worldview.

NINETY-NINE

JIM

"Brother helped by brother is a strong fortress." (Proverbs 18: 19)

Nicolas, nearly two, is presenting a growing challenge to his big brother. When Nicolas was smaller, Alexander's casually dismissive attitude—"Oh, he's a baby (followed by a dismissive wave of the hand or a not so gentle push if the second born was within easy reach); now let's play!" This worked fairly well since the "baby" couldn't do that much. But now Nicolas is talking and walking, and he is game to imitate anything he sees or hears. He is shrewd enough, mostly, to avoid going head to head with his big brother. As a result, he has become the master of the kind of indirection I've heard about in the martial arts, where you let your opponent fritter away his own energy by letting him lunge harmlessly past you. Watching the smaller boy dance around his confused big brother, I think of Muhammad Ali's "Float like a butterfly, sting like a bee!"

This kind of footwork is, of course, harder to manage in the back seat of a car, especially since Nicolas is elaborately strapped into a car seat and Alexander is in an age-appropriate seat and shoulder belt contraption. There are sometimes fiercer conflicts in those constricted circumstances, with me usually in the middle. But now that Nicolas talks rather than crows, Alexander no longer insists on wearing headphones so that he won't be deafened by his brother's excited squealing. I think I detected something new, though, on my last visit with them. Every once in a while I heard, not the usual rhythm of silence-smackshriek, but some low-pitched dual giggling. I didn't tell their parents, but I think I detected the first signs of collusion. Instead of regarding each other as encumbrances or objects of torment, it was beginning simultaneously to dawn on both of them that, if they joined rather than divided their forces, they could make their parents truly crazy.

And why not? They're both smart and charming, and the three-year-age difference won't matter that much down the road when they're ready to take on the world. It'll be interesting to watch their enterprises grow. My brother, who has been there, says that the true Survivor years are *teen age*. I suspect Hank is right even though he doesn't have a million dollars to prove it.

ONE-HUNDRED

Ruth

"Experience, travel—these are an education in themselves."
(Euripides)

When parents, children, and grandparents live at a distance, the phone and letters become extremely important. Sending messages by e-mail or fax works for adults, but children are not print oriented, so direct contact by phone or in drawings and personal writings in better. All the grandparents whom I know spend a lot of time selecting appropriate greeting cards for all occasions and writing simple, personal messages in them. When they receive back a card with scribbles somewhat forming the child's name, they are just as proud of this as they would be of a perfectly formed and orderly group of paragraphed words.

A brief three-minute conversation by phone to hear my grandchildren's voices and what is happening at that very moment is a real treat. Just last week Nicolas told me enthusiastically about sleeping for the first time in a big boy's bed. Alexander especially likes to tell me about riding his bike, a skill that I helped to teach him, or about any type of fall resulting in a scratch, cut, or bruise. But many times Alexander, a typical male, just doesn't want to talk at all.

In an attempt to spark enthusiasm for communicating back and forth by mail, Alexander and I have often shared a fun book called *The Jolly Postman or Other People's Letters* by Janet and Allan Ahlberg. This book introduces in rhyme a mail carrier on a bike. He is delivering letters to various addresses. The first one is from Goldilocks and is for the three bears. The letter itself is in an actual envelope. It is written with inventive spelling and has small, carefully drawn pictures to help the nonreader understand the text. Goldilocks includes a postscript at the end of her letter. I took advantage of the opportunity to explain its meaning and use the first time we read it together, and we talked about the fact that all the letters had different addresses. Every time we get to the page with the envelope in subsequent readings, he focuses on it and has to take the letter out. He likes the stamp on it because it shows a king with a pipe in his mouth. Children today aren't used to seeing these. Even Santa seems to have joined the non-smokers. The first time we read *The Jolly Postman*, I had to explain what a pipe was. Another postcard has a picture of an airplane and the words *par avion* written underneath. Alexander, unlike me, now repeats these words with perfect enunciation. It wasn't too long ago that he came back to this page many times during each reading to study the plane and make engine sounds instead.

    Living on the West Coast, Alexander and Nicolas have flown to the Midwest many times to visit us. Their other set of grandparents lives on the East Coast, a full day's travel from Vancouver. Both boys have been to France to see relatives, especially their great, great grandmother, who is alive and well in her nineties. They have already spent more time in the air than I have over my entire lifetime. At very young ages my grandsons, like many other children today with spread out families, have had many chances to travel. Just because the new generation has opportunities doesn't mean that it automatically learns from them though. Communication and geography skills still must be taught.

    Come to think of it, Nicolas, who is just at the age when little boys like to make airplane noises, has never heard *The*

Jolly Postman. It's a good thing that my next visit with him is only four weeks, five hours, and twenty-six minutes away.

Printed in the United States
1665